FAITH
WORKS

Jim Wallis is a commentator on ethics and public life and a spokesperson for faith-based initiatives to overcome poverty. He is the editor of *Sojourners* magazine, covering faith, politics and culture for 30 years. He is also the convener of Call to Renewal, a national federation of churches, denominations and faith-based organizations working to overcome poverty and revitalize American politics. A frequent speaker, he travels to more than 200 events a year to preach, teach and organize. He is a prolific writer whose columns appear in the *New York Times*, *Washington Post*, *Los Angeles Times*, MSNBC and Beliefnet. His previous books include *Who Speaks for God?*, *The Soul of Politics* and *The Call to Conversion*. He also regularly offers commentary and analysis for radio and television. Jim lives in Washington, DC with his wife Joy and their son, Luke.

ALSO BY JIM WALLIS

Who Speaks for God?
The Soul of Politics
The Call to Conversion
Revive Us Again
Agenda for Biblical People

EDITED BY JIM WALLIS

Cloud of Witnesses
Crucible of Fire
Waging Peace
Peacemakers
The Rise of Christian Conscience

FAITH WORKS

Lessons on Spirituality and Social Action

JIM WALLIS

Published in Great Britain in 2002 by
Society for Promoting Christian Knowledge
Holy Trinity Church
Marylebone Road
London NW1 4DU

Original edition published in the United States of America by Random
House, Inc., New York and simultaneously in Canada by Random
House of Canada Limited, Toronto in 2000

British Library Cataloguing-in-Publication Data
A catalogue record for this book is available from the British Library

ISBN 0-281-05525-4

Typeset by FiSH Books, London WC1
Printed in Great Britain by Antony Rowe Ltd, Chippenham, Wilts.

Contents

To my mother, Phyllis Ruth Wallis,
who showed me in her life and in her death
how faith works.

And to my wife, Joy Carroll Wallis,
who turns the walk of faith
into a dance of life.

A Word About This Edition

WHEN I WAS A BOY, Robin Hood was one of my heroes. Now I tell my three-year-old son Luke stories of Sherwood Forest and the Merry Men who took money from the rich and gave it back to the poor from whom it had been stolen. Economic redistribution has always seemed like a good idea to me. When I came of age and found my own faith, it was the Hebrew prophets and Jesus who always held the most appeal: 'Let justice roll down like waters,' thundered Amos; and in his opening Nazareth manifesto, Jesus proclaimed a gospel that is 'good news to the poor'.

So it was with a sincere opening line, in my very first British speaking tour in 1980, that I declared that Robin Hood had always been my favourite English theologian. It wasn't my first time in Britain but my first real trip around the whole country, and it became the occasion on which I fell in love with my British cousins. For a whole month we travelled in a van across the length and breadth of England, Scotland and Wales, stopping most nights for a large rally or revival meeting in a town hall, cathedral or church. From enthusiastic Liverpudlians who reminded me of American black church audiences, to very earnest and socially conscious students in Cambridge, to down-to-earth working-class Christians in the Midlands, to fervent Afro-Caribbean Pentecostals in east London, to passionate Scots and Welsh who made me think of my own heritage, I was meeting people to whom I would stay connected for the rest of my life.

During that unusually hot June, the battle for freedom in South
Africa was at a critical point, and we spoke of it at every venue.
I've always appreciated how Britain is so much more
internationally inclined than my native America, where no news
organization ever really matches the depth and breadth of the
BBC. Britain would eventually adopt sanctions against the white
regime in Pretoria long before the US, and, in so doing, help bring
about the end of apartheid. I remember discussing South Africa
during a very warm meeting in Birmingham with the Anglican
clergyman Barney Pityana, the exiled South African leader who
was the close associate of the black consciousness prophet Steve
Biko. But we also spoke of 'urban ministry', which has been such
a part of my life and which some British churches were starting
to pioneer. Racial justice and reconciliation were also a central
theme of the tour, and I began to compare notes with black and
Asian leaders about the similarities and differences between
British and American racism. Those discussions have continued
through the years.

At the heart of the preaching of that first tour was the idea of
'radical discipleship', a term that was near and dear to my first great
friend in Britain – the radical Scot Jim Punton of Frontier Youth
Trust. What he meant and I meant was that following Jesus would
inevitably turn you into a radical – radical regarding the biblical
imperatives of the kingdom of God. Over the years, I've met many
radical Christians in Britain. I've often worked with members of the
Iona Community from Scotland, and have been enriched by their
deep sense of worship, service and justice. Like my own
ecumenical community of Sojourners, Iona has brought people
together from across the theological spectrum. I will also always
treasure the times spent in Northern Ireland with Iona's sister
community, Corrymeela, where Catholics and Protestants found
unity together and where the promise of today's ceasefire in that
troubled country was quietly nurtured. Community itself was a
theme of that first tour, and one place our little van took us to was
the Post Green community in rural Dorset, where good friends like
Jeanne Hinton, Tom and Faith Lees, and 'the Fisherfolk' sought to
live out the message of spiritual and social renewal.

There have been many trips to Britain since that first tour, but
none more momentous than the one in the summer of 1994 when
I came to speak at Greenbelt, that creative and cutting-edge festival
of arts, music and Christian social conscience. I had often spoken

at Greenbelt, but this time I was put on a panel next to a very attractive and articulate young Anglican priest named Joy Carroll. The topic was 'What's the point of being an "evangelical"?' Some people told me that she was 'the real Vicar of Dibley', but I had no idea what that meant. That Greenbelt encounter proved to be life-changing for me, as it eventually led to a trans-Atlantic romance, a happy marriage and a little boy who loves to listen to stories about Robin Hood in the dark just before he goes to sleep. Of course, Luke is a dual-citizen now with deep family roots in both countries. He has even learned to be bilingual, pronouncing words like 'bath' and 'tomato' or saying 'trousers' or 'pants' just like Mummy or Daddy as it suits the occasion or his agenda. He regards Britain as home too and we will forever be a transatlantic family.

Joy and I disagreed about that panel topic, and we still do! I regard myself as an 'evangelical' but of the kind who roamed England in the eighteenth century, like John Wesley and John Newton, or, in the nineteenth, preached spiritual revival and social reform across America. These Christians were vocal for the cause against slavery, fought for the protection of child workers and helped establish women's suffrage. For them there was no division between the sacred and the secular. They knew that history is changed by social movements with a spiritual foundation.

Those movements are as contemporary as today's news. I have been an American spokesperson for Jubilee 2000, the powerful faith-inspired movement, begun in Britain, that led to the cancelling of much of the debt that has crushed the world's most impoverished countries. When I had the opportunity to meet the Chancellor of the Exchequer, Gordon Brown, he told me, 'No movement has impacted Britain as much as Jubilee 2000 since Wilberforce led the anti-slave trade campaign.'

That is the theme of this book – how to build spiritual and social movements that can change the world. That is my calling and my work. And I still do it with many British partners, like my good friend and long-time collaborator Bishop Peter Price, who wrote the foreword to this book. My British cousins are really my family now and, over these two decades, many of us have become brothers and sisters in the mission to put our faith into action. *Faith Works* tells that story in our modern world, and I am very grateful to SPCK for publishing the British edition.

Foreword

JIM WALLIS AND I first met in 1980. I had been through a particularly bruising experience of community, but I had discovered during a retreat I was making on the Island of Cumbrare some copies of *Sojourners*, the magazine Jim has edited for 30 years. It was to prove life-changing. I began to understand the need for connections to be made between faith, politics and culture. At the time, Jim Wallis and the community at Columbia Heights in Washington, a few blocks away from the White House, were seeking to bear witness in the aftermath of the civil rights marches, and the struggle for racial equality among America's minority ethnic citizens. Through their community, and their magazine, the Sojourners were endeavouring to speak truth to the powerful on a range of issues – the nuclear menace, women's rights, poverty and wealth, just economics, as well as the then conflict in Central America.

Sojourners magazine became a monthly 'pick-me-up', helping me to read the Bible with fresh eyes, as well as to understand the connection between faith and action in a way that led me to comprehend that if we pray for God's 'kingdom to come', we must also work for its coming. Such discipleship means being prepared to challenge the forces of oppression and discrimination that all too easily dominate our lives.

Jim and I have become firm friends over the years, and I have been privileged to contribute as a writer to the magazine, as well as to share with Jim over many aspects of his 'activist preaching'. What I have found inspirational about this latest book, *Faith*

Works, is that it continues Jim's commitment to making faith work in all kinds of practical activity. But Jim isn't an 'answers' man; he believes in the value of listening to our questions, and from our questions addressing how we practise faith. Sometimes that faith practice will demand things from us that we never believed we could do – at other times it will call on us to dance!

This book tells the story of a man who has walked the walk as well as talked the talk. What you see is what you get. Here is someone who has lived the gospel as well as preached it. Here you will find the story of Jim's conversion, but you will also discover how conversion is for him both a present moment and a continuous experience. You will listen to him talking with gang leaders, archbishops, presidents and students. Over the years, despite many set-backs and difficult times, here is someone who has kept the faith and remained a man of hope. Here is a realist, but not a cynic. Here is someone who believes in the ultimate triumph of the grace of God. Discipleship is taking up the cross, but the grace and power of God in Christ is revealed through the empowerment of the Holy Spirit who makes us sufficient for these things.

I had the privilege of preaching at his marriage to Joy Carroll, one of the first women priests in the Church of England who, on a lighter note, has provided much of the inspiration for BBC Television's *The Vicar of Dibley*. The wedding was joyous, as indeed is the home that Jim and Joy share in Washington with their son Luke, who shows every sign of following in Mum and Dad's footsteps. This 'activist preacher' has been around for a few years, but he offers us not only inspiration to ensure that 'Faith Works', but also measures his life in the joys of new-found love in family life. I hope you find true in this book one of Jim's favourite sayings: 'Hope is believing in spite of the evidence, then watching the evidence change.'

+Peter B. Price
Bishop of Bath and Wells

Acknowledgements

MANY PEOPLE HELPED make this book possible. My long-time editor and old friend, Roy Carlisle, persuaded me it was time to write a book about how 'faith works', and my wonderful agent and friend, Gail Ross, with her brilliant book sense, helped create the idea. Roy's tested wisdom and experience shaped the project all through the writing.

I am also grateful to the American publishers of *Faith Works*, Random House and my editor, Susanna Porter, who published the hardback edition; and PageMill Press, led by Roy Carlisle, who published the paperback edition. I'm very pleased that SPCK, with my very competent editor, Alison Barr, is releasing this edition.

The Center for the Study of Values in Public Life at the Harvard Divinity School invited me to join them as a Fellow for the 1998–99 academic year, which provided me with the perfect opportunity to write the book. At Harvard, my extraordinary research assistants, Emily Dossett and Michaela Bruzzese, gave invaluable help with research, and Emily also became a trusted editor. Duane Shank, my policy adviser, worked tirelessly carrying out the necessary research, tracking down critical information, which he does like nobody else. Erin Card, my executive assistant, worked with her characteristic competence and grace to coordinate events around the release of *Faith Works*.

So many friends and colleagues from Sojourners and Call to Renewal contributed by reading the manuscript, commenting on my ideas, serving as dialogue partners, telling me stories, and working on the same visions and projects. I'm grateful for their feedback, counsel, ideas and example. They have shaped my thinking and this book more than many of them know. But the responsibility for what the book says, and how it says it, is mine.

For the inspiration, sustenance, companionship and editing suggestions that made the writing so much more possible, I thank my wife, Joy Carroll; and for constant delight throughout long book-writing days, I thank my son, Luke. For the faith that undergirds this book, I thank my mother, who died while it was being written, and my father, who continues mourning, but still believing.

A Personal Word

MY MOTHER DANCED at our wedding. Given the prohibitions on dancing in my evangelical upbringing, that was a pretty big deal. Joy and I took it that my parents were quite happy about our getting married. Mum could have passed for a woman 15 years younger and looked positively vibrant as she whirled around the floor of the Anglican parish hall in south London. She and my father combined the marriage celebration in Britain with a much anticipated month-long holiday in Europe. They were very happy and healthy, and life was good – wonderful, really.

Almost a month later, my mother discovered that she had cancer of the stomach lining. Thus began a long battle, fighting the disease with a combination of conventional surgery and chemotherapy with alternative treatments of vitamins, serums and an extremely healthy diet. At one point she was drinking so much organic carrot juice that she turned orange! My mum was so strong and determined that she survived a heart attack and heart surgery twice, and then the agony of shingles tested her even further – all seemingly consequences of the cancer and its treatment.

Learning that my wife, Joy, was pregnant, and that she would soon have a new grandson, my first child, seemed to give my mother added incentive to survive, and even to get better. After Luke arrived, she was absolutely thrilled to get to know our son and her thirteenth grandchild. I never saw her happier than when she held Luke in her lap, and he gave her all those generous smiles of his. Then my mum was excited to learn that her youngest daughter, Marcie, was expecting a new baby in May 1999, the day before her own seventy-fifth birthday. On she battled, looking more and more healthy after each set-back.

But on 30 April I got a call from my brother, Bill, in Detroit. My mum had collapsed at home. She had an infection in her bloodstream. Four out of five cancer patients die from something other than cancer because the body has been weakened so much. However, the doctors and my dad seemed optimistic at first; she had always pulled through before. But three days later we got another call. My dad's voice sounded emotional and scared. 'You'd better come.' We flew from Boston just hours later. Now the doctors feared she might not live through the night. My sister Barb and I got to the Detroit airport at the same time from different parts of the country and hurried to my mother's bedside. When we got there, the first thing she said was to ask my dad whether he had got fresh milk for us back at the house and whether he had put clean sheets on the beds. Some things never change.

That very day, my sister Marcie made a bold move. Already in the early stages of labour, my youngest sibling decided to get in the car and drive three hours with her husband and three boys from western Michigan to Detroit, to be with her mother. Marcie had her medical records faxed to the hospital Mum was in and got there in time to visit her before checking into the maternity wing of the hospital, called, ironically, the Miracle of Life Center. The whole family was there now (five brothers and sisters and lots of grandchildren) to hope and pray for a miracle...that Mum would live to see her new grandchild. Marcie told us the secret she had kept for months – it was a girl.

On the morning of Mum's seventy-fifth birthday, 6 May, Marcie went into serious labour. They were two women on a mission: as my mother laboured for her life with each breath, Marcie laboured to bring forth new life. It seemed as if we almost lost my mum twice, but she was determined to hang on. Marcie had previously had distressed deliveries with all of her boys, but this time her labour was smooth and quick. She knew what she had to do. The doctor who delivered Marcie's baby commented that he had never seen a woman more in touch with her body and more in control of her labour. There was not a sound in the delivery room during the whole ordeal.

At 1.35 p.m., Kaylee Ruth was born on the first floor while her grandmother Phyllis Ruth lay dying on the fifth. As soon as they could, the doctor and nursing staff wheeled Marcie and the baby into Mum's room, where we were all waiting so anxiously. The jubilation was overwhelming. The whole hospital had been following the drama, willing these two special people to meet and bending the rules for newborns. As my mother opened her eyes and held her new granddaughter, she smiled and said, 'I'm very happy, I'm very happy.' Those were her last words before she slipped into a coma. Both the doctor and nurse who helped Marcie deliver were in the room with us now, with tears in their eyes just like all the rest of us. The veteran obstetrician later remarked to the head of his unit that he had never been involved in so remarkable a birth story.

My mother's coma lasted another nine days. Now under hospice care in the hospital, she never came out of the coma, but was responsive the whole time, especially to my father, who never left her side. One morning he said with some alarm to the nurse, 'Her hand is warm!' She replied, 'Well, you've been holding it all night!' I stayed in the room round the clock for several nights until he seemed ready and eager to be alone with the woman he had been with since they were both 16. 'We had some good long talks last night,' he would say when I brought him clean clothes each morning. The long vigil was a challenge but proved to be a gift for my father, who later said that he needed that time to be able to let her go. The nursing staff treated my mother wonderfully during her last days. One of them said, 'We all really care about her.' They kept asking if there were any more babies coming or family holidays that were keeping her going! My mother was never afraid to die during her year and a half of sickness and never even complained about it; now she was showing how tough she really was. My theory is that she was still enjoying my dad's companionship too much to go quickly. And she always loved to have all her children and grandchildren around her. She was the centre of our attention.

My mother passed away at 12.15 a.m. on 15 May 1999. My father, who was at her side, as he had been each day during this last two-week hospital vigil, said she went 'calmly, peacefully, and beautifully'. He called me, and I called my brothers and sisters, who were there in Detroit to be with her. We all went to the hospital to be with my mum and dad for an hour before we gathered up her things and brought my father home.

My mother's memorial service drew almost five hundred people, and the little church she and my father had helped to found had never been fuller. Women in the church from her generation always had to lead from behind the scenes. Even so, my mother was so widely known and loved that more people turned out for her memorial than for any other event in the church's 50-year history. The tributes and testimonials went on for three hours, and would have gone on much longer had my dad not finally said it was enough.

How did she find the time to do all those things for all those people, I wondered, and still make each one of her children and grandchildren feel so special? I realized it was simply the way she and my father treated people, and especially anybody in trouble or need, that had planted a strong social conscience in all her children. She taught us principles: if there is someone nobody is playing with, you play with them; if somebody is getting picked on, you defend them; never make fun of anyone for any reason, and don't ever be cruel to people. I didn't want my mother ever to catch me being mean to someone. Finally, she and my father always taught us to stand up for what we believed, no matter who disagreed. That last one would be tested when we kids would later apply the principles they taught us and make social and political commitments that were new and challenging to them. But even then, there was always support for their kids and, eventually, a good deal of agreement with them.

After a family burial service, out-of-town family headed home. Joy and Luke and I went back to Boston, where we had been living for a year as I was trying to finish this book. Now we'd all try to go back to our normal lives – with my mother's memory and legacy, but without her presence. My mother's obituary, printed in the Sunday *Detroit Free Press*, ended with these words: 'She is remembered by her family, church, and friends around the world as a loving wife, devoted mother and grandmother, minister of hospitality, and exemplary woman of God.'

Our family witnessed the grace of God over those two and a half weeks and the mystery of life and death, literally side by side. The grieving over my mother's passing and the joy over Kaylee Ruth's birth filled our hearts with tears of sorrow and joy. I have never experienced a more vivid illustration of death and resurrection bound together by the love of family and the love of God. It filled the hospital room so powerfully that many doctors and nurses commented on it. This hope of life in the midst of death is the very centre of faith; in fact, it is what faith is all about.

Such times of great emotions and stress seem to focus many aspects of life and faith and test the meaning of both at very deep levels. They also bring back memories long forgotten but suddenly vivid. One for me was a simple prayer my mother taught me as a little boy, which I found myself praying with her as we kept a vigil with her night after night. It is a simple but strangely reassuring prayer.

> *Now I lay me down to sleep,*
> *I pray the Lord my soul to keep.*
> *If I should die before I wake,*
> *I pray the Lord my soul to take.*

Our prayer always went on to list all the people we prayed for each night and ended with a regular closing line that my mother must have found a necessary one, 'And help Jamie [that's me] to be a good boy.' I told her I would keep trying.

The vigil with my mother and the birth of Kaylee Ruth taught me important lessons about faith and how it works. I saw the primacy of love and the strength of fidelity. In the end, love is the measure of life. What happened with my family for two weeks in that hospital room, and what I saw between my mother and father, was simply a love story and a testimony to faith. In the testimonials to my mother from so many, I was reminded how teaching and living the most basic principles of kindness, compassion and service are what finally draw people in to love and give authenticity to faith – it's what makes faith human. I was dramatically reminded of the risk taking, exemplified by my sister's courage, that always accompanies true faith. And I literally experienced how hope and life are always born anew, even in the midst of the deepest pain and grief. The mystery of faith is that life and death are always concurrent. Indeed, life comes out of death. That is the promise and power of faith.

My mother's death came in the midst of my final work on this book. Suddenly, the vigil with my mum and the book writing became deeply connected. In this book, I invite you to reflect with me on what faith means for our world today. The book will ask what it means to stand up for what you believe and how your beliefs can be put into action. So come with me on a journey.

Introduction

The Difference That Faith Makes

Faith without works is dead. (James 2.26)

HOPE IS BELIEVING in spite of the evidence, then watching the evidence change. That's what I've learned after almost three decades of working for change as a person of faith. People often ask me, 'Where have you found the strength to stay involved for so long?' or 'How have you stuck with it and not burned out?' I've asked those questions myself. But more often I've asked myself how I can make the most difference in the world. For me, the answer to both questions is the difference that faith makes. What do I mean by faith? I like the definition used by the biblical writer of the Letter to the Hebrews: 'Faith is the substance of things hoped for, the evidence of things not seen.' Simply put, faith makes hope possible. And hope is the single most important ingredient for changing the world. It has continued to provide the energy and sustenance I've needed, not just to keep going but to be continually renewed.

Now you know and I know that religion has not always played a positive role in the world. I think sometimes God must get very embarrassed by some of the things we human beings say we do 'in God's name'. Tragically, religion has too often been a sectarian and terribly divisive force. In places like Northern Ireland and Bosnia, the battles are often disguised as religious, when underneath the conflicts are economic, cultural, ethnic, nationalistic and always political. Religion is often used as a sword to divide, rather than as a balm to heal. And religious leaders and institutions can be guilty of the kind of power-politics tactics that tear people apart instead of bringing them together. Toward one another, the different religious communities sometimes behave no better than rival street gangs.

Any audience reading a book like this will be full of people who have had bad experiences with religion. Let's face it, most of us have. I felt virtually kicked out of the little church I was raised in when, as a teenager, I was made to feel very unwelcome. Lots of us know how it feels to be unwelcome in religious institutions. But that experience didn't cause me to lose my faith for ever, and I hope others don't throw theirs away either.

I could be as sceptical as anyone about faith and religion. I probably know more about the sad side of the religious story than most. But I haven't stayed in that sceptical and cynical place, and here's why: I have also experienced the promise and power of faith. When slave masters put the Bible in the hands of their slaves, it was meant to control them, to turn their eyes toward heaven and away from doing anything about their plight on earth. But in that book the slaves found Moses and Jesus. Their faith became the foundation for their liberation, and its spiritual power enabled them to keep their eyes on the prize. I can say that too. I know the oppressive and divisive side of religion, but I've also found the transforming power of faith that can change lives, neighbourhoods and nations. I have a long history in the streets and in the places in this world where suffering is most intense. I've seen that suffering, but I've also seen the faith that can prevail in and through it.

In a public forum at Harvard's John F. Kennedy School of Government, I was challenged by a student who feared the danger of religion to human rights and couldn't see past the horrors of places like Bosnia. I didn't argue with her. I admitted that our history is full of such examples, and those on the inside of faith communities have the biggest obligation to be critical of religion gone bad. If we cannot acknowledge the reality of the darkness, we can give no credence to the power of the light. I gave my assent to her concerns, but then I told her it was my own identity as a Christian that most persuades me to care for the world. For me, my faith is what has consistently pressed me to search and work for the common good.

This book is full of stories about people who have acted on that positive vision of faith. Instead of divisive, they have found faith reconciling; instead of wounding they have found it healing;

instead of debilitating, they have found it empowering; instead of creating more obstacles, they have found a faith that removes them. There is an enormous practical wisdom in these stories, and a compelling reason for faith.

The Test of Faith is Action

Many people today are hungry for spirituality but have no appetite for religion. Still others, who are part of religious communities, are asking how their faith might be connected to the urgent problems of their world. But spiritual interest may no longer be enough. In today's world, the test of any authentic faith is action.

Much of life is a matter of faith, especially the parts that count the most. At the beginning of the new millennium, the spiritual is overshadowing the political as a preferred solution to social problems. The future promises to deepen the relationship between faith and politics. The biggest question is: Which will transform the other?

Perhaps the greatest heresy of twentieth-century American religion was to make faith into a purely personal matter and a private affair, which went neatly with the rise of the consumer society. With the advent of the television preachers, faith was turned into an occasion for conspicuous consumption and effective fund-raising. Faith became merely another commodity: 'I have it, and you don't.' Or worse: 'Here's how you can get it too. Our operators are standing by!'

In the Bible, faith is not something you possess, but rather something you practise. You have to put it into action or it really doesn't mean anything. Faith changes things. It's the energy of transformation, both for individuals and for a society.

The Bible begins with the creation story – how God created the world and all its creatures, including us. From the beginning, the venue of faith is the world, what's happening in it, and how that squares with God's intentions. How these creatures are interacting with one another, the rest of Creation and their Creator is the heart of the biblical drama. The place where we look to find the face of God is our life in the world. With God so interested in the world, it's a wonder that contemporary religion has often seemed so uninterested.

As recently as the eighteenth and nineteenth centuries, both Britain and the United States experienced revivalist faith as a catalyst for great social movements, such as the abolition of slavery, child labour reform, and women's suffrage. In the last century, American black churches led the way in the civil rights movement by putting faith into action for freedom.

It took a lot of faith for those early civil rights activists to endure the hatred and violence of the system of racial discrimination. It also required a change in the nation's moral climate and values to end that system. Changing the entrenched pattern of racial segregation in the American South, ending apartheid in South Africa, or tearing down the Berlin Wall seemed virtually impossible before they happened. People had to really believe such things could be done before they were possible. That 'believing' is the essence of faith and the beginning of any change. You must believe the change is possible before it ever will happen. Indeed, every important social change begins with some people believing it is possible. Hope always precedes change. Hope is the substance of faith and the only absolutely indispensable ingredient for individual and social transformation. I've learned that there is a spiritual chain of events in history: faith–hope–action–change.

It wasn't very long ago that few people held any real hope for change in South Africa. And it wasn't until I met with 14-year-olds in the black townships there that I became convinced of freedom's eventual victory. I saw that the children had decided something – that their country would be free. Change always begins with some people making decisions based on hope, and then staking their lives on those decisions. The difference between optimism and hope is that the former changes too easily; the latter is rooted in something much deeper. That something is faith. South African archbishop Desmond Tutu always said that people of faith are 'prisoners of hope'. The succeeding events in his country vindicated that faith.

Perhaps my favourite story of the power of hope comes from a memorable moment shared with Desmond Tutu in South Africa. I love to tell the story about the extraordinary drama I witnessed at St George's Cathedral, in Cape Town, where the Nobel Peace Prize winner and Anglican cleric preached. A political rally had just been cancelled by the white government, so Bishop Tutu called for a worship service instead, inside the beautiful cathedral. The power of apartheid was frighteningly evident in the numbers of riot police and armed soldiers massing outside the church. Inside, all along the cathedral walls, stood more police openly taping and writing down every comment made from the pulpit. When Tutu rose to speak, the atmosphere was tense indeed. He confidently proclaimed that the 'evil' and 'oppression' of the system of apartheid 'cannot prevail'. At that moment, the South African archbishop was probably one of the few people on the planet who actually believed that.

I had been clandestinely sneaked into the country to support the South African churches during a time of great crisis, and to report their story back in the United States. This was the first day of my six-week stay, and I had just arrived from the airport. Now I sat in the cathedral congregation and watched Archbishop Tutu point his finger right at the police who were recording his words. 'You may be powerful, indeed very powerful, but you are not God!' And the God whom we serve, said Tutu, 'cannot be mocked!' 'You have already lost!' the diminutive preacher thundered. Then he came out from behind the pulpit and seemed to soften, flashing that signature Desmond Tutu smile. So – since they had already lost, as had just been made clear – South Africa's spiritual leader shouted with glee, 'We are inviting you to come and join the winning side!' The whole place erupted, the police seemed to scurry out, and the congregation rose up in triumphal dancing. I had the blessing to be at Nelson Mandela's inauguration and to have some moments with Archbishop Tutu. He smiled when I reminded him of that day at St George's. I said, 'Bishop, today they've all joined the winning side!' They had indeed.

Perhaps we have reached so many personal and political impasses in America and the West because we have failed to recognize the moral and spiritual character of our problems. Yes, religion has too often been the occasion for dividing people into sectarian gangs and warring factions. But faith can also be the spiritual energy that enables the transformations for which our world so desperately hungers.

Many people today would like to find some way to practise their faith or spirituality, despite the excesses, corruption or narrow regulations of religion that have turned them away. I believe the making of the modern Christian, Jew, or Muslim will be through action. When put into action, faith has the capacity to bring people together, to motivate and to inspire, even across former dividing lines. We demonstrate our faith by putting it into practice and, conversely, if we don't keep the power of faith in the actions we undertake, our efforts can easily lead to burnout, bitterness, and despair. The call to action can preserve the authenticity of faith, while the power of faith can save the integrity of our actions. As the biblical apostle James put it many years ago, 'Faith without works is dead.' Indeed, faith shows itself in works – faith works.

Where We're Going

All through the book, I share my own life experiences and other stories from around the world that inform the chapters and give them a very human reality. But there is also a spirituality that runs throughout the book, and I've chosen a biblical text that expresses the heart of that spirituality. The text is from Chapter 58 of the biblical Book of Isaiah. Isaiah was a Hebrew prophet of the eighth century BC who laid out a vision for a good society. Still used extensively by both Jews and Christians today, Isaiah's wisdom reminds us that our own fulfilment in life is bound up with our neighbour's well-being. Only in reaching out to our brothers and sisters, especially those in most need, will we find our own best humanity. It is a spirituality in which everyone benefits and a new sense of community is the result. I believe it is a spirituality for our times. I hope that this insight we gain from Isaiah undergirds the whole book. So I would like to offer Isaiah's prophetic words here, at the beginning of the book, and invite the reader to use them as a meditation throughout the reading. Use the text as a touchstone, and Isaiah's wisdom will become more and more apparent as you move through the stories that shape the book. Don't just read, but hear the words of the prophet.

Is not this the fast that I choose: to loose the bonds of injustice, to undo the thongs of the yoke, to let the oppressed go free, and to break every yoke?

Is it not to share your bread with the hungry, and bring the homeless poor into your house; when you see the naked, to cover them, and not to hide yourself from your own kin?

Then your light shall break forth like the dawn, and your healing shall spring up quickly; your vindicator shall go before you, the glory of the Lord shall be your rear guard.

Then you shall call, and the Lord will answer; you shall cry for help, and he will say, Here I am.

If you remove the yoke from among you, the pointing of the finger, the speaking of evil, if you offer your food to the hungry and satisfy the needs of the afflicted, then your light shall rise in the darkness and your gloom be like the noonday.

The Lord will guide you continually, and satisfy your needs in parched places, and make your bones strong; and you shall be like a watered garden, like a spring of water, whose waters never fail.

Your ancient ruins shall be rebuilt; you shall raise up the foundations of many generations; you shall be called the repairer of the breach, the restorer of streets to live in. (Isaiah 58.6–12)

This is *not* a book to tell you one more thing you have to do. Instead, it offers a vision of how everyone in the community can become more healthy, healed and whole. It makes the vital connection between service and spirituality, which is key to our future. From that connection flow all the 'lessons' to change your world and heal your soul – here are practical lessons in what to do and how to do it. I hope readers will make another connection – between reading a book and joining a movement.

Chapter One

Trust Your Questions

Who is my neighbour? (Luke 10.29)

EVERY NEW DIRECTION in one's life journey begins with some new questions, and so did mine.

I was just another white kid from everything that was 'middle' about America. We were from Michigan. We were middle-class. We were Christians. We lived in a nice suburban Detroit neighbourhood, and my brother and sisters and I all went to good schools. The world looked fine to us. My parents believed that we lived in the best city in the best state in the best country in the world.

My father graduated from the University of Michigan, was commissioned as a naval officer, and got married all on the same day in June 1945. The government was anxious to get him and a fresh contingent of sailors off to the Pacific to help end the war. My mother had been strong enough to win his heart and win him over to her Christian faith. After the war, my parents settled their little family in a new three-bedroom house, in a neighbourhood full of returning World War II veterans with families just like ours – all financed by the new Federal Housing Administration.

I grew up with an abundance of warm affirmations, constant kudos and great expectations for success. The first of five children, I was 'saved' at six and baptized at eight in the little evangelical church my dad and mum helped to establish.

I won't easily forget the night of my dramatic childhood conversion. A fiery evangelist had come to our church for a Sunday-night revival service, and all the kids were asked to sit in the very front rows. I felt as if the preacher was pointing his finger right at me when he said, 'If Jesus came back tonight, your mummy and daddy would be taken to heaven, and you would be left *all by yourself.*' Well that was sobering, especially when I realized that, as a six-year-old boy, I would have a five-year-old sister to support! That very night, I quickly asked my mother how I could be saved, being quite ready to repent of the sin and degradation of my first six years. But to her everlasting credit, she didn't talk to me about God's wrath but told me how much God loved me. That sounded great to me, so as best as I understood how, I gave my life to Jesus. Things went smoothly from then on. Good grades, sports and youth group activities were my life's priorities. In fact, everything was going very well until some questions began to form in my head and heart as I became a teenager.

Questions of the Heart

I asked questions first in my own world of family, church and school. In that world, everybody's dad had a job, dinner was on the table every evening, and only bad people that our family didn't know ever went to jail. We weren't rich (with five kids in the family, we spent most of our vacations camping at state parks in Michigan), but I had never met anyone whom I would call poor. But increasingly, I was hearing and seeing things that troubled me. On the news and in the papers, I was hearing more about inner-city Detroit, just a few short miles away. I read stories about unemployed fathers, hungry families, and overcrowded jails. Then there was this new civil rights movement in the South, and some minister named King.

Minister? The church where I grew up was literally the centre of our lives. I wondered why the only black faces I'd ever seen in my church were on the missionary slides from Africa that we sometimes watched on Sunday nights. Weren't there black churches in Detroit? Why hadn't we ever visited one or invited their members to our church, as we did with lots of other white Christians? In Sunday school, I had been taught to sing:

> *Jesus loves the little children,*
> *All the children of the world,*
> *Red and yellow, black and white,*
> *They are precious in His sight,*
> *Jesus loves the little children of the world.*

I supposed that was true about Jesus, but I could see it wasn't true of the white Christians around me.

My high school government classes also taught me that in America, all people 'are created equal'. But as I listened to many of the white citizens of Detroit, I discovered that they didn't really believe that. Why was there such resistance among my classmates at our all-white high school when our young English teacher had us read a book about racism and talk about it?

My world was safe and secure, white and middle-class, and full of easy answers. But new questions were arising in the early 1960s. I was just a teenager, but something didn't seem quite right. That's often the beginning of the process, the start of a journey – something doesn't seem quite right.

My questions were these: Why was life so different in 'white Detroit' than it was in 'black Detroit'? Why were so many people in the inner city without good jobs or decent houses? Why were there hungry families in the United States of America? Why were so many young black men in jail? While starting to look at the world around me, I also began to ask what our Christian faith said about the racial attitudes I was discovering. Why did we have no contact with the black churches? What did they think of us? Weren't we all supposed to be part of the 'body of Christ'? After the questions began, things got difficult. When I raised my questions, I could feel the cool distance between me and many of the people around me, even those I had been close to since I was a little boy. Then the arguments came, in school, in church and at home. The arguments were hard on all of us.

Some people told me I was too young to ask such things, and when I got older I would understand. Others admitted they didn't know why things were this way either, but it had always been like that. The only really honest answer I got was from a church elder who told me, 'Son, if you keep asking these questions, you're going to get into a lot of trouble.'

That turned out to be true. Probably the most important decision I made at that time was to keep asking my questions until I got some answers. I recommend that. Follow your heart, trust your questions, and pursue them until you find answers that satisfy you. How questions get put into our heads and our souls is a great mystery. I still don't know why these questions intruded into the mind and heart of a successful teenage kid mostly preoccupied with sports,

grades, church youth groups and, of course, girls. All I know is that
the questions were there and wouldn't go away.

These questions of the heart, as I like to call them, are an
entry-way into our own spirituality. They beckon us to a deeper
place and a more honest life; they are a call to conscience and,
ultimately, an invitation to transformation. The religious would
say that God puts those questions in our hearts; others might say
they are a link to the spirit within us. The most important thing
is that the questions be diligently followed; to turn away from
them is to turn away from the voice of your own conscience
and, perhaps, the voice of God.

Pilgrimage to Detroit

My pursuit of the questions took a teenage white kid from the
suburbs into the inner city of Detroit. And there a whole new world
opened up to me. As pilgrimages go, the one I made from the white
suburbs to the inner city of my own town was a very short one –
only a few miles. But it felt as if I was moving from one world to
another, because I was. Was I scared? Sure, a little. But I also had to
find out what was going on around me. I tried to find chances to
connect to the city. After I got my driver's licence, at 16, I would head
downtown, find somewhere to park, and just start walking around.

I found myself wandering the streets of downtown Detroit.
There I was, exploring a world very different from mine, strangely
compelled by the 'inner city', which everyone warned me to
avoid. The homeless vagabonds, prostitutes and young street kids
were as intrigued by the sight of me as I was by them. I knew the
people I grew up with would be terrified and horrified. Why was
I there? I wasn't really sure. But the city drew me like a magnet.
Life seemed more real there, more human, and more interesting
than in the suburbs, which now felt artificial and isolating to me.
The diversity also drew me. Where I lived and went to school and
church, everyone was like us. In contrast, and in spite of all the
differences, I felt somehow connected to the people in the city,
felt that we were all related in some way that we just couldn't
understand. I remember feeling that it was important to try to
figure that out.

I also began reading, mostly books by black authors. One was
a book entitled *My Friend, the Enemy* by a young black Christian
named Bill Pannell. He was from the same little denomination of

churches that I was, the Plymouth Brethren, but from the group's black congregations. I had never known they existed. Bill's little book was about his very ambiguous relationship with his fellow white Christians. I found it fascinating, and since he lived in Detroit, I went to hear him speak. And what I heard him say made all the sense in the world. I knew that I was hearing the truth, and I was finally getting some answers to my questions.

Because of my church background, I started going to black churches. I really liked the sermons and loved the gospel choirs from the first time I ever heard one. People were always friendly and inviting, and I began to meet people who could answer my questions. It wasn't always direct; I didn't 'interview' anyone, I just watched, listened and asked people about their lives. I've always felt welcomed in the black churches and still do to this day. Maybe that's why the black church has always been a spiritual home for me. Of course, the answers to some of my earnest and eager questions were obvious, but I never felt patronized or dismissed. Listening to a good black preacher and a good gospel choir is always a very satisfying experience, one that I highly recommend. And you will always be welcome. What I found in the black churches was a lively faith, but one connected to a world very different from the Detroit in which I had grown up. And this different world was becoming clearer to me every day.

As I got ready to go to college, and then all during my university years, I took summer jobs in the city, putting me alongside young black men my age. From them I learned that we had grown up in two different countries, yet only a few miles apart. On factory assembly lines, where the temperature would regularly climb to over 100 degrees, we had hot conversations about the world that would radically change my perceptions of it.

The Motor City was a racially divided town, a fact that became dramatically clear to the nation in the hot summer of 1967 when Detroit exploded into riots. I was there and felt my heart inflamed along with my city. The urban disorders that shook Detroit were blamed for polarizing the city. But in reality they simply revealed the deep racial polarization that was already there. Why were most of the white people around me so unwilling to look underneath the 'riots' to find the reasons for them? I didn't understand everyone's defensiveness to all the questions that were growing in my head and heart. But I also recognized that some of the racial stereotypes I had learned as a white child were still inside me. I realized that I had a lot to learn, and to *unlearn*. So I made sure I got my own paperback copy of the famous Kerner Commission Report into the causes of the 1967 disorders and studied it diligently. I read the thick, well-documented report several times, until the pages became dog-eared. And through it, I learned how difficult it really was for America's black citizens to find 'life, liberty, and the pursuit of happiness'. I pored over the report's statistics on education, employment, housing and police behaviour, which revealed a nation, said the Kerner Report, 'moving toward two societies, increasingly separate, and dramatically unequal'.

The young men I was meeting were militant and angry, and as I listened to them I became angry too. During this same period, I first read *The Autobiography of Malcolm X*, written with Alex Haley, and I discovered that the young Malcolm had also spent some time in Detroit. Now I was beginning to see some of the life of inner-city Detroit that had so shaped 'Detroit Red', as Malcolm X was formerly known.

One person I've never forgotten is Butch, a black co-worker in a downtown office building who taught me many lessons about life. We worked together as caretakers, furniture movers, and substitute lift operators. He was smart, and he always had a book sticking out of the back pocket of his khakis. But he wasn't going to university like me. Our paycheques had different destinations – mine to a college savings account, his to support his mother, brothers and sisters, and young wife.

On the days we ran the lifts, the company was legally required to give us extra breaks so our heads wouldn't start to spin. But on my breaks, I often rode up and down with Butch in his lift, and on his-breaks, he rode with me, so we could talk about politics. Our heads did begin to spin, but not just from the ride: rather, it was from what we were learning about each other's world – our families, neighbourhoods, schools, hopes, dreams and futures. I quickly learned that Butch knew much more about my world than I knew about his.

Meeting Butch's mother was an experience I'll never forget, and one I've come to realize was pivotal in my own pilgrimage. She wasn't especially political, and certainly not militant. But like my own mother, she loved her firstborn son and was afraid his radical ideas might get him into trouble. Because her husband had died young, she relied on Butch a great deal. During my visit, the youngest of Butch's brothers and sisters climbed right up into the lap of this strange white guy, with trusting smiles on their faces. The older ones held back, showing much more suspicion. It's a pattern I've often seen since. It doesn't take long for the experience of racism to erode childlike innocence and trust.

What I most remember from that first meeting, though, was a conversation in which Butch's mother related the experiences the men in her family had had with the Detroit Police Department. She told me the advice she gave all her children regarding the police: 'If you ever can't find your way home and seem to be in a strange neighbourhood, watch out for the police. If you see a policeman, quickly hide down a stairwell or behind a building. Just don't let him find you! After he passes by, it's safe to come out and find your way home.' In Detroit, I had heard stories about the reputation of the white police for brutalizing young black people. But as Butch's mother spoke, my own mother's advice to me and my brother and sisters on the same topic rang in my ears: 'If you're ever lost and can't find your way home, *look for* a policeman. He is your friend and will bring you home safely.' Moments like that are truly converting experiences that stay with us for the rest of our lives.

It was my questions that led me to the inner city, to the black churches, to Butch's living-room. Those questions eventually led me to the decision to become involved in the civil rights movement as a college student. Detroit was my early baptism of fire, teaching me how racism had betrayed the ideals I had been taught as a child. Another lesson I learned is that we are terribly diminished without our ideals, and the struggle to protect them is absolutely crucial to our integrity as persons and as a nation. That struggle always depends on asking the hard questions.

One Question Leads to Another

When I was a college student, the war in Vietnam was escalating, and so were the questions of a new generation. Vietnam became another classroom for a whole generation of Americans like me. My high school girlfriend's cousin Don and several other young men I knew were sent over there. Don had got into trouble, and the judge said he could choose between jail or the Marines. Back home, I got teargassed more times than I can count in peaceful demonstrations against the war, many of which I helped organize. One day, Don and

I compared our experiences of Vietnam and realized we and our whole generation had all become veterans of the war, one way or another, some fighting in it and some fighting against it. The war shaped us all. Again we were criticized for raising questions, but it was the hard questions that finally shone a light on US policies in Indochina and the logic of a war that degenerated into 'destroying a village to save it'.

As a young adult, I experienced the successes and failures of the student movements of the 1960s. During my college days, at Michigan State University, we learned how to put 10,000 people in the street in a few hours' time, but also how such a powerful movement could quickly collapse into moral confusion. I remember the first time anti-war protesters began smashing downtown store windows in East Lansing, Michigan, I wondered what was happening to us. I saw the dangers of hating your country (as some anti-war protesters came to do) instead of loving it enough to try to correct its mistakes. I questioned how a movement for peace could degenerate into bitterness, violence and even hatred. I began to learn that it's easier to criticize your government's policy than to ask tough questions of yourself.

But I remember Martin Luther King, Jr, explaining his opposition to the war in Vietnam. 'I oppose the war,' he said, 'because I love America. I speak out against it ... with anxiety and sorrow in my heart, and above all with a passionate desire to see our beloved country stand as the moral example of the world. I speak out against this war because I am disappointed with America. There can be no great disappointment where there is no great love.' King's opposition to the war was like the anguish of the biblical prophet Jeremiah, hurt by the sins of his people yet proclaiming the justice of God.

My experiences as a movement organizer were raising a number of deeper issues. Racism, poverty and war had motivated my earlier questions. But what were the spiritual roots of social change? Was there a moral foundation upon which to build new political visions? Can political ideology alone answer the deepest longings of our hearts or resolve the problems of our public life?

My early disillusionment with the Church had caused me to lose my childhood religion. But was I now finding my way back to faith? I began to look at Jesus again – or perhaps for the first time. I started reading the New Testament again, which I hadn't done in many years, just on my own. What I began to see in the first three

Gospels was a Jesus who stood with the poor and marginalized and who taught his followers to be peacemakers, a Jesus I had never heard much about in church but was now rediscovering. I read Jesus's Sermon on the Mount, which lays out the priorities of a new way of life in a new order that he called the kingdom of God. In this new order, the poor would be blessed, along with those who were moved by human suffering, who were merciful, who were gentle in spirit but hungry for justice, who were people with integrity, who were peacemakers, and who were persecuted for just causes. Somehow, I'd missed that in church.

But it was the twenty-fifth chapter of Matthew's Gospel that really caught my attention. In a scene of final judgement, Jesus asks the people who assume they are his followers how they have treated the hungry, the thirsty, the homeless strangers, the naked, the sick and the prisoners. The question startles them, especially when he suggests that he has been all these things and they have not ministered to him. His would-be disciples are incredulous. 'Lord, when was it that we saw you hungry or thirsty or a stranger or naked or sick or in prison, and did not take care of you?' Jesus's reply astounded me. 'Truly, I tell you, just as you did not do it to one of the least of these, you did it not to me.' Here Jesus was so identifying himself with the rejected and excluded of the world that to serve them was to serve him, and to ignore them was, indeéd, to ignore him. I had never heard anything as radical as that, certainly not in all the revolutionary literature of the time that I was reading. It was humbling, too, for a self-confident student radical to realize that his life needed some changing. I knew more than ever, then, that I didn't have all the answers, but trusting my questions was still taking me to new places.

I decided to go to theological seminary in Chicago. There, I began to make the connection between faith and action that I mentioned earlier and that would become the foundation for my life and work. I began to learn that spiritual values could teach us much about the human condition while giving us new visions for social change. Hearts had to be changed as much as policies, and that was an even deeper challenge. I remembered that the civil rights movement, rooted in the black churches and a very powerful spirituality, was far more successful and morally centred than the youthful white student movements of the same period. Seminary was also where I began to learn the importance of community, about the problems and possibilities of living and working together with other people.

Community was where we learned about ourselves and how much transformation each of us needed if the world was truly to be a better place.

In seminary, several of us began a little magazine, which I'm still involved with today. In each issue, *Sojourners* addressed the two topics you aren't supposed to discuss in polite conversation: religion and politics. And we committed the even greater offence of trying to put those topics *together* – today our masthead still reads, '*Sojourners* – Faith, Politics, and Culture'. We thought that church and state should remain separate, but that moral values and public life ought to be connected.

Always, asking new questions led to wider involvements. During the 1980s, I learned how to mobilize churches around the country on a myriad of social issues. For example, the religious community became the animating core of a movement alerting the nation to the dangers of the nuclear arms race. We helped initiate the nuclear freeze campaign that brought in even wider constituencies. Our allies spanned the gamut from Carl Sagan to Billy Graham.

Questions about justice, peace and faith can inevitably lead you beyond your own borders and to more questions. During the years of war in Central America, many of us made the pilgrimage south. I learned firsthand about the ravages of war on the northern frontiers of Nicaragua, where we took busloads of volunteers down dusty rutted roads with mortar shells shooting over our heads, seeking to create a new campaign called Witness for Peace amid cold-war-inspired violence. We ultimately sent 5,000 North Americans to Nicaragua to work for peace. Holding your pack over your head while crossing overflowing rivers in the Philippines, stumbling through rice paddies, sleeping in hammocks covered with mosquito netting, and celebrating the Eucharist on altars decorated with candles in Coke bottles will also raise many questions about your comfortable way of life back home. Having clandestine dialogues with Soviet dissidents in Moscow before Communism collapsed jumbled up the old Left–Right categories, made me rethink my political assumptions and deepened my commitment to genuine democracy. And meeting with aboriginal leaders in the Australian bush taught me new lessons about the arrogance of dominant cultures. Everywhere I went, I continued to learn the value and power of asking questions.

It's always the deeper spiritual questions that have such a capacity to change us. Keeping one step ahead of the security police in black townships, I got to know South African church leaders like Desmond Tutu, who deeply believed that one day their nation would be free. I experienced the power of hope as I never had before as black South Africans made believers of the rest of the world. I will never forget a day that transfixed the planet – 10 May 1994 – when I stood with 150,000 cheering South Africans sharing tears of joy at Nelson Mandela's inauguration. It was one of those rare days when you can see and feel the world changing right before your eyes. Everyone spoke that day of 'the miracle' that was occurring. Such a powerful event was humbling, reminding me that the really important changes surpass all of our individual efforts and tap a spiritual power that causes us all to be amazed by grace.

Failures also teach many lessons, as I learned in 1990, when a small group of American church leaders tried in vain to find a way to peace in Baghdad on the eve of the Gulf War. We seemed to persuade some members of the Iraqi cabinet that withdrawal from Kuwait would be far better than seeing the children of Baghdad bombed, but Saddam Hussein wanted war, as did George Bush. We felt we had failed. We came home and organized a service of more than 8,000 people praying for peace in Washington's National Cathedral on the night before the bombing began. Despite our best efforts, the war proceeded and most of the nation rallied around the CNN coverage of the quick US victory. The peace movement was demoralized, and I became aware of how much my own ego had become invested in the quest for peace. A personal 47-day fast, embarked on during the days of war that followed, probably taught me more about the deeper spiritual challenges to real peace than most of my organizing ever had. I saw more clearly than I had before that 'peace' really does begin with me.

Spiritual Power

Today, we publish *Sojourners* magazine in Washington, DC, but it's not the Washington with which most people are familiar. In the 'other Washington' people are not wealthy and powerful but poor and politically powerless. I live in Columbia Heights, about 20 blocks from the White House, where children who inhabit the

inner city in the capital of the world's last remaining superpower
sometimes go to bed to the sound of gunfire and experience
violence, drugs and despair as their daily norm. It's still a revealing
question to ask why this is so. Our little Sojourners Neighborhood
Center has for 20 years been a safe place and a beacon of hope for
at-risk children and their parents, in what otherwise has often
seemed like a war zone. Working with those kids, we try to practise
what we preach, and through them we have learned close up the
realities behind the problems that the city's media pundits
ceaselessly debate from far above the fray. Living and working
here has been an invaluable education for me, as well as a vital
spiritual discipline. It continually raises new questions about how
people, families, communities and nations really do change – or
don't.

My neighbourhood has constantly given me a perspective that
I would not otherwise have had. Once, I returned from a meeting
at the White House about youth violence only to find the
infamous police yellow tape on the pavement right across from
my house, indicating where another young man had just been
shot and killed. I remember reflecting that most people who
attend such meetings don't come home to places like this.

Moving to inner-city Washington to work in the shadows of the
nation's Capitol revealed a tale of two cities – a pattern I began
to see internationally through increasing travel around the world.
Everywhere, there was an upper city and a lower city, and the
relationship between the two tells you much about a society.
Asking questions about the lower city teaches you how things
really are (especially for those at the bottom), rather than just
what the people at the top say about their society. In most places
I go, I try to be sure to visit both cities.

I'm on the road a great deal, so I get to know the most hopeful
people and projects in America today and in many places around
the world. Mostly, I try to help nurture and inspire what I think is
the most important force for changing the world, or at least our
own corner of it – namely, social movements with spiritual power.

Speaking from 200 to 300 times a year for more than two decades,
and to audiences of all kinds, I've come to know America pretty
well, and other parts of the world too. I've had the opportunity to
travel to thousands of American cities, towns and communities, and
hundreds of places internationally – always speaking and listening,
encouraging and being encouraged, mobilizing and seeing how

people are organizing themselves. But it's always people's questions that interest me most. People often tell me that I'm at my best when responding to people's questions after my speeches. That's probably because I enjoy the questions so much and think they're so important.

Our questions are often shaped by where we're asking them from. Our vantage point is critical. My view of the world has always come from very diverse vantage points – from lovely hotel windows to dirty housing project balconies, from university lecture halls to homeless shelters, from the corridors of political power to the muddy roads of poor shanty-towns, from the nation's great pulpits to the insides of assorted jail cells, where I've been sent probably 20 times by now for various vigils, marches and peaceful actions of nonviolent civil disobedience. I've noticed how different the world looks from those different places.

The many examples of social change I've seen along the way have been a grounding for my visions of how the world might be different. I've had the blessed opportunity to be instructed and inspired by the very best efforts in the land and around the globe that are helping to turn our world in a better direction.

I've seen what really changes the world, what finally makes a difference. I've discovered that the world can be changed; we just have to learn how, and we have to begin close to home. And I would say the most important lessons I've learned have to do with the energy and power that come from bringing moral and spiritual values to public life. A spiritually rooted approach to social change not only offers good models for solving problems, but contributes what is perhaps the most valuable commodity in the struggle to genuinely transform our world: the presence and power of *hope*. It's often faith that makes hope possible, and when hope is present, new things begin to happen. So often, the most important question to ask is simply: Where can we find the hope here?

A New Table

Sometimes I've been able to help bring various efforts together or help people find common ground they didn't believe was possible. I've helped facilitate both gang peace summits and religious roundtables that brought warring factions to the table. The 'table' has been a constant metaphor and tactic for me, a place to form new connections, ideas and partnerships.

Always asking the question of how to put faith into action can land you in some unusual places and circumstances. In the early 1990s, for example, I became involved in supporting some of the gang truce movements that were emerging. One Sunday morning in 1993, I found myself sitting in a black Baptist church in Kansas City, Missouri, after a weekend Gang Peace Summit. In a congregation that included a couple of hundred former and current gang members from all over the country, I was reminded of how far I had travelled from the white suburbs of Detroit, Michigan. But on that morning, there was nowhere else in the world I would have wanted to be; I felt privileged to be there 'at the table'.

I'll never forget what happened that morning. Two young rival street warriors, who had been trying to kill each other all that past year, dramatically dropped their gang colours in the pulpit and resolved from then on to walk together on the road to peace. There wasn't a dry eye in the house. My tears were also for churches who couldn't or wouldn't come together for the sake of their communities, the way these young men and women were doing. It was that morning when the idea came to attempt a similar truce between the churches. If some Crips and Bloods can do this, why not the evangelicals and liberals, the Catholics and Protestants?

Just like the young gangsters, the churches would need a reason to come together, after years of acting like gangs themselves in their battles over turf, money, and power. Everyone knew the churches *ought* have more unity, but as was the case with the street gangs, it would take a crisis to provoke a new coming together, one that people would feel deeply.

That crisis and opportunity came when Congress and the White House virtually ended the nation's 60-year-old social welfare system in the autumn of 1996. Almost everyone agreed that the old welfare system wasn't working very well and certainly wasn't overcoming poverty. But the politicians ended it without first putting alternatives in place. That caused a shudder in the religious community, which, as a historic and major service provider, was now afraid that too much of the burden would fall on it. But at the same time the churches were sensing fresh responsibilities and even a new commitment.

Several colleagues and I decided to take a risk by calling together a summit of our own. Almost 60 church leaders gathered together at a new roundtable and for nine hours talked and prayed through the issues. After one of the most remarkable days any of us could remember, a new unity began to be forged. A vision of partnership began to emerge, first for the churches and then for other organizations and leaders in local communities. It was a unity for the sake of poor people who were facing a potential crisis greater than any in years. It seemed that the poor were bringing the churches together.

With the old welfare system gone, a whole new set of questions was now being asked. One was how to create the necessary alternatives before all the welfare cuts were put into place. That effort would take the involvement of the whole community – the churches, nonprofit organizations, businesses, unions *and* government officials. Our guiding principle was that every group should do its part, and each would do what it does best. The solutions we needed now wouldn't conform to the old categories of liberal and conservative, Left and Right. Instead, we committed ourselves to forge a new kind of moral and community politics where *values* would be more important than *ideology*. One of our central affirmations was that the way to find common ground is to move to higher ground. We named the new effort Call to Renewal to indicate that the task would be as spiritual as it was political.

I agreed to be the convener of this new federation of faith-based organizations – churches and religious groups with faith at their centre – who are trying to overcome poverty. We began to organize town meetings and roundtables around the country, where new questions and challenges were creating new partnerships. The 200 town meetings we did in the first two years convinced me that a new era of multisector cooperation is indeed possible, with pastors and nonprofit organizations coming together with elected officials, police chiefs, and leaders in the business community and workforce to create strategies and to mobilize resources for community change.

Call to Renewal holds the promise for a movement of faith in action that brings together many constituencies from the religious community and beyond. At a Washington press conference, the evangelical leader Rich Cizik hopefully proclaimed, 'The cold war between religious groups over the poor is now over!' Again, new questions were creating new possibilities.

What with *Sojourners* magazine and the home front, travelling and speaking, teaching, and now Call to Renewal, life is busy. But I have never felt more potential for significant change, precisely because more people are recognizing the spiritual dimensions of serious cultural and political transformation. Young former gang leaders speak of the 'spiritual power' necessary to overcome 'the madness' of urban violence. Religious leaders confess that their former divisions have hurt poor people. Elected officials are exploring the benefit of partnering with faith communities, and a variety of civic leaders are ready to build new alliances and find new answers based on common values. Legions of students are having transforming experiences as they move out from their campuses to volunteer their time and energy as an expression of their spirituality. Pastors and members of congregations are trying to find ways to become better involved in their communities. People from all walks of life are trying to find meaning and morality, not only in their personal and family lives but also in their work and vocations. Most important, ordinary people with jobs and kids are discovering that trying to make a difference in their own communities may be the best way to heal their own souls. People are trusting their questions and letting the questions lead them to new places.

Over the last three decades, I've experienced many large social movements and small local projects, neighbourhood ministries and national coalitions, political campaigns and political protest, both victories and defeats, and with each one there have been lessons learned.

The journey begins by trusting your questions. Other lessons follow from that.

Chapter Two

Get Out of the House More Often

You are the salt of the earth . . .
You are the light of the world. (Matthew 5.13–14)

THERE IS A STORY about a young priest who was very nervous about his new responsibilities. He was especially worried about leading the Eucharistic liturgy. The priest has to say the right words in the right order – for instance, 'The Lord be with you', to which the congregation duly responds, 'And also with you'. The new cleric was concerned that he might foul up his parts of the liturgy, causing the congregation to get their parts wrong too. The whole thing might fall apart, and he would feel like a failure. So you can imagine the young man's panic when he got up before the gathered parish that first Sunday morning, only to realize that his microphone had gone dead. Frantically, the rattled priest began to tap his finger hard on the silent microphone and exclaimed, 'Something is wrong with this microphone.' The congregation replied, 'And also with you!'

I sometimes start with that story when I'm on the road speaking because it's always fun to begin with a good laugh. But the story also helps me introduce my next point. After the laughter dies down, I suggest that *something is wrong in our society*, and that most people feel it – all across the political spectrum. At that point, the heads begin to nod in agreement.

Despite the constant claims by politicians, Wall Street's elite and the media pundits about what 'good times' these are, most people sense that some things have gone wrong at the moral core of our society. Something about our values just doesn't seem right, and sometimes things really seem to be unravelling. But what is actually happening to us, and why, and what can we do about it? That we're not quite so sure about. To figure it out, we are going to have to understand our problems at a deeper level. Raising questions is a good start, but we soon have to decide how far we're going to pursue the answers. To go further, we need to get some new perspectives. We learn that we can't just take this journey in our heads. We have to reach out to broaden our experience, to move beyond familiar places, and even to cross boundaries we never have before. So our second task is to 'Get out of the house more often!'

The Journey Begins

To change our world, or our community, we first have to understand it. To understand it usually requires a change in our thinking. And for that to happen, we have to experience more of the world than we can know inside the comfortable confines of our lives. We have to cross the barriers that divide people and, indeed, that separate whole worlds from one another. Most of us are deeply programmed not to venture past those invisible but powerful signs that silently scream at us: No Trespassing! You shouldn't be here! You don't belong here! It's not safe! You won't be accepted! Stay where you are!

But I've found that those very powerful cultural messages are usually false, designed in part to keep us from seeing and experiencing people and parts of life that may change our perspective. It's not a big conspiracy; rather it's an ingrained cultural conditioning that keeps people in their own world and prevents them from experiencing another one.

Most of the people I've met who are deeply committed to social change will trace their own transformation to the time when they first went to a third world country, or even just across town to the inner city. There, in a world very different from their own, they had conversion experiences that would shape the rest of their lives. It wasn't so much reading a great book or hearing an inspiring lecture that changed them but rather their *experience* in a war zone, a refugee camp, a youth centre, a women's shelter or an urban church trying to hold a community together. Time studying at the university can, ultimately, be less educational for social change than time spent on a reservation, in a ghetto, in a barrio or in a mountain hollow.

When I talk to people about how change really happens, the

first thing I try to impress upon them is that it is both *possible* and *worth it* to cross the normal boundaries of our lives, to escape our comfort zones and experience a different reality. That's always the first step. You can stay at home and keep accepting the easy answers, or you can step out and make some new discoveries. If you don't get out, you'll never know what's really going on; if you do, a whole new world opens up.

And it's the more in-depth, longer-term experiences outside of your own world that can have the most lasting impact. My wife, Joy, is an example of that. At the age of 18, she spent a year working in the countryside of Haiti, the Western Hemisphere's poorest nation. Taking a year off before college, she plunged into a world very different from anything she had ever known. Joy had grown up in the working-class neighbourhoods of south London, but she had never seen poverty such as she encountered in Haiti.

The actual work she did was for a project to bring clean and safe drinking water to people in a rural area. There is probably nothing more taken for granted in developed countries than clean water; yet the lack of safe water is a leading cause of disease and death all around the world. It is estimated that more than five million people, including two and a half million children, die each year from illnesses related to unsafe water and improper sanitation.

Living and working with some of the poorest people on earth for a year had a profound effect upon this English schoolgirl. Joy was for ever sensitized to the plight of people at the bottom, those who are always shut out and left behind. Later, she became a priest in the Church of England. But she always stayed in the inner city and paid special attention to people who are poor, homeless, mentally and emotionally disabled, aged, immigrant or outcast. Something got into her blood in Haiti, and it's never left her. Now she talks about starting a new church for the poor in Washington, DC.

You also won't really know yourself if you stay inside the carefully constructed boxes of your life. Getting out of the house is actually the first step on a spiritual journey; take it and your life will begin to change. That is both the promise and the challenge. Only by the challenges encountered in stepping out do you learn what resources you have and what contribution you can make. What you gain is self-understanding as well as spiritual awareness. The path of self-discovery is critically linked to the process of social and political transformation. But the first step is to walk outside of the old, familiar places.

Putting a Face on the Poor

My friend Joe Nangle, a Franciscan priest, often speaks of Olga, a
poor woman he met while working in Peru. One day, Joe helped
Olga bury her nine-year-old son in a paupers' graveyard; the boy
had been killed by a hit-and-run driver and then denied dignity by
a system that didn't care what happened to the children of poor
families. 'That day for ever changed my relationship to Olga, and in
some ways for ever changed me,' Joe says. 'Perhaps for the first time
I really saw what life is like for the poor – for that two-thirds of
humanity who live as Olga lived, who bury their children as she
did. From then on, and increasingly, Olga Valencia came to
represent for me the literally billions of people, especially women,
whose lives can hardly be called human. When I wanted to put a
name and a face on "the poor", it was invariably Olga's name and
Olga's face.'

But priests aren't the only ones learning to see the poor. I met
Dale Recinella in 1998 and soon learned about the extraordinary
journey this middle-aged man and his family had been on. An
international lawyer from Florida who made a high-six-figure
income in the 1980s, Dale had decided to devote his energies and
substantial skills to helping overcome poverty. Previously, he had
arranged the financing on multimillion- and even billion-dollar
deals for corporations, banks and governments. Now he wanted
to put together multisector partnerships to help move families out
of poverty. But it all started with the awkward involvement of a
high-priced lawyer in a soup kitchen. Dale tells the story of how
he began to change. Like many others, he saw some of the
problems around him and decided to get involved. He had no
idea what he was getting into or how it would change him. Dale's
recounting of his life-transforming experiences is compelling.

'Almost seven years ago, I started helping out at the noon meal
of the Good News Soup Kitchen in Tallahassee. I showed up
every day in my three-piece suit to help from 11 a.m. until 1.30
p.m. They assigned me "door duty". My job was to ensure that the
street people lining up to eat waited in an orderly fashion. Every
day, I stood at the door for an hour, chatting with the street
people waiting to eat. Before I came to Good News, "street
people" was a meaningless term. It defined a group without
defining anybody in particular. From the comfort of my car, my
suburban home, and my downtown law office, street people were
just "those people out there somewhere".

'Then one day an elderly woman named Helen came running to the Good News door. A man was chasing her and threatening to kill her if she didn't give him back his dollar. "Tell him he can't hit me 'cuz it's church property!" she pleaded. In true lawyerly fashion, I explained that Good News is not a church but he still couldn't hit her. After twenty minutes of failed mediation, I bought peace by giving each of them a dollar.

'That evening, I happened to be standing on the corner of Park and Monroe. In the red twilight, I spied a lonely silhouette struggling in my direction from Tennessee Street. "Poor street person", I thought, as the figure inched closer. I was about to turn back to my own concerns when I detected something familiar in that shadowy figure. The red scarf. The clear plastic bag with white border. The unmatched shoes. "My God", I said in my thoughts, "that's Helen".

'My eyes froze on her as she limped by and turned up Park. No doubt she would crawl under a bush to spend the night. My mind had always dismissed the sight of a street person in seconds. But it could not expel the picture of Helen. That night as I lay on my fifteen-hundred-dollar deluxe temperature-controlled waterbed, I couldn't sleep. A voice in my soul kept asking, "Where's Helen sleeping tonight?" No street person had ever interfered with my sleep. But the shadowy figure with the red scarf and plastic bag had followed me home. I had made a fatal mistake. I had learned her name.'

That's what happens when you get involved. You learn people's names, and that makes all the difference. Poverty is no longer just a social or economic problem when you have a personal friend who is poor. Gang violence is not just a law-enforcement issue when you've spent time listening to a kid tell you why he has taken to the streets. 'Welfare mother' is no longer a term of derision when you've gone over the budget of a woman who's trying to raise her kids on $410 a month. Personal involvement seems to defy the easy answers while at the same time it opens up the possibilities of real solutions.

It is just that sensitizing that the world so desperately needs. Joy Carroll, Joe Nangle, Dale Recinella and I were all brought up in comfortable homes. None of us would have learned what we eventually did if we hadn't got out of the house. It has a way of changing your perspective, as Joe says ... for ever.

It's precisely that change in perspective that will make the most difference. And if you have in your mind the picture of a friend's face from the inner city of Detroit, a young child in Haiti, a refugee family from El Salvador, a grieving mother in Peru or a homeless person on the streets of Tallahassee, it's easier to find the right perspective. I've learned many things about what really changes the world – and what makes a difference. Mostly I've learned that the world can be changed; we just have to begin by getting out of the house.

A Fair Test

The Jesuit Volunteer Corps, which sends young people into inner city and rural poverty areas for a year of service, has a wonderful motto: 'Ruined for life!' Their simple idea is that once you've seen real poverty and got your feet wet by doing something about it, you won't ever be the same again. After that service, you may indeed go on to other things, but that year of hands-on involvement will change your perspective, they are convinced. And so am I.

My brother, Bill Weld-Wallis, coordinated the Jesuit Volunteer programme in the Midwest for a decade and tells heartening stories of how most of his alumni have gone on to live lives of community service through their career, family and personal choices. These were all ordinary people. They weren't activists or clergy or community leaders. They were just volunteers. What's most significant is what they became. Service is only the beginning; it's the transformation that comes from service that is the critical ingredient for personal and social change.

When I speak on college campuses, I often spend time with the students who are volunteering their time and energy in the community or around the world. I remember such an evening at a small college in central Texas. Before I gave the evening lecture, I had dinner with several of these young people who had decided to get out of the house. Some had just been to an international conference on peace in the Middle East and were planning to go back to work there for a year. Others had been to South Africa to serve in the efforts to build a new country free of apartheid. Still more had travelled to Central America to help with the shaky peace processes in those countries.

Virtually all of them had been extensively involved in volunteer projects throughout the United States. The conversation just crackled with energy and excitement. They had already learned so much, had so many more questions, and were hungry to keep going. Their experiences had already caused many of them to change their courses, and they were hoping it would change their lives. One could easily tell that these young people had come a very long way from the familiar worlds of suburban and rural Texas where most of them had grown up.

After my talk, we retreated back to the campus chaplain's house and continued the discussion. I challenged them. When I was their age, I told them, we could put 10,000 people in the street in two hours' time. In response to the civil rights movement and the Vietnam War, we became a generation forged in protest. Their generation had now also taken to the streets, not so much in protest as in volunteering. We marched in the streets for change; today's youth work in the community in order to make a difference.

The test of what my generation did, and what today's students are now doing, I suggested, is simply this: Will what you are doing change the direction of your life? My generation has often failed that test, and the test results for this generation are not yet in. If volunteer projects become merely the preoccupation of a few student years, to be forgotten when the larger life choices are made, little transformation will have occurred. But if this work changes the life trajectory of people, and shapes their most basic choices about faith, vocation, family and money, especially in the most formative period of their lives, then real change will have begun. The students all thought that was a fair test, but a tough one.

One person who wants to change the lives of young people is Bart Campolo. He's the director of Mission Year, a rapidly growing youth volunteer programme that is affiliated with Call to Renewal. Mission Year recruits college students to give a year of their time either before or after graduation. They move into an inner-city neighbourhood to work with a local church. Their plan is simple and powerful. The young people go from house to house, asking whether people would like them to pray for the needs of that home. Most of the people they call on say yes, many probably thinking 'What could it hurt?' Sometimes the students pray right there on the doorstep or are invited into the house. But in the course of the prayer, the circumstances and needs of the people in that house are often made apparent. Aware of those needs, the students are then able to help people make connections to other sources of support or assistance.

My generation – the baby boomers – have become the biggest consumers in history. Many of the old dreams and ideals have faded. Reality set in, and many compromises were made. Having once stepped out for change, many are now safely back within comfortable boundaries. Those who got more deeply involved in the organizing in the 1960s, and not just the marching, tended to feel the more lasting consequences. It is the depth of one's involvement that seems to make the most difference.

Now the members of my generation are stepping into positions of leadership throughout society. And many are remembering the formative influences of their student years and recalling commitments we once made. One hears more and more stories of people in successful careers deciding to do something they think more meaningful or important. I have increasing numbers of conversations with people in my generation who wish to somehow recapture the ideals they once professed but have gradually forgotten. Among my generation of now middle-aged professionals, a new spirit of community involvement may also be in the air. If a reawakening of conscience began to occur among a new generation of leaders, in partnership with a younger generation hungry for service, exciting new possibilities for change could emerge.

Start by Doing Something

We've become used to a pattern of public discourse that has become quite dysfunctional. A problem is stated, an argument erupts about its causes, the blaming begins, the rhetoric rises, the confrontation is joined and quickly becomes partisan – and nothing is ever done about the problem. There is another approach. A problem is stated. The various dimensions of it are described as best we can understand them. Then a strategy is conceived for *involvement* with the problem in the hope of finding the necessary solutions. Instead of rushing to theoretical debates, various community leaders and institutions begin to engage the situation, believing that a diverse set of people and resources will probably be necessary to solve the problem.

In the first process, the community or the nation gets further divided while no answers are found. In the second, the community is strengthened in a cooperative effort, and positive progress is more likely to be made.

In other words, the best way to begin solving a problem is to start by doing something. It's a simple notion, so simple it often escapes us. In the process of involvement, not only will likely solutions begin to emerge, but everybody involved may be changed by better understanding what is really going on. This more helpful process is starting to occur as more people choose to address problems in their communities by getting involved in them.

Integrity is also something that seems to be found in personal involvement, even if you're unsure how to proceed. I think people are more and more tired of those who profess to be experts on so many problems but have had little personal involvement in trying to solve them. Talk is cheap, as they say. Taking action doesn't provide panaceas, but at least it wins respect for actually trying to do something. Is it any wonder that Jimmy Carter is much more respected as former president than he ever was as president? When you ask people why, they don't speak of the impressive Carter Center in Atlanta; rather they conjure up the image of the former president pounding nails into a new house for a poor family on a Habitat for Humanity work project. And Mr Carter is a serious builder, too, not a politician looking for a good photo op while painting over graffiti for 30 minutes in front of the network news cameras. I've been on one of the Habitat sites with Carter and seen how he doesn't tolerate idle conversation when there are houses to finish!

We have to dispel the myth that you really have to know what you're doing before you start doing it. Just accept the fact that you're going to make some mistakes. Everybody does. But that's the way we learn. The Sojourners Neighborhood Center didn't begin as a successful freedom school. We started, 25 years ago, by tutoring children who ended up on our front steps. We did it in our living-rooms. None of us was an experienced tutor, but we'd all been to school. Training is vitally important, and we've done a lot of it over the years. But you've still got to start somewhere, and you'll never get the experience until you just begin.

We started *Sojourners* magazine in much the same way. We were all seminary students who became powerfully moved by the idea that faith should show itself in action and that spirituality was vitally connected to politics. We had a message and needed a vehicle. Someone suggested that we start a magazine. None of us had ever done that before, but we were young and bold enough to think that we could learn. So without any journalistic experience, we launched a new publication. Our first mailing list came from a brainstorming session one night, and our first distribution strategy was one car heading east and one west with a new magazine hot off the press.

I've always likened publishing *Sojourners* to running a flag up a flagpole. Many other people at the time were also wanting to put their faith together with a commitment to social action. But they didn't know one another; they couldn't see one another on the ground. But when they saw that flag raised in the form of a new magazine, they headed to the flagpole, where they all met. That was the beginning of a constituency, a network, and a movement for faith in action that has grown until this day. And it all began with lifting a banner high enough for people to see it.

That's how change often happens, in a community or in a nation. Someone has to lift up a banner, and other people stream to it. Change often requires a catalyst, an occasion, an event or a new initiative. Someone has to start something, and others will become involved. You may be the one to lift the banner, or you may be one of the crucial people to join in and help hold it up. At the beginning, you never feel ready, and you hardly ever know what you're doing. But you begin anyway, because change has to start somewhere.

Back Home

One night, my father was out at a church elders meeting when I called, so my mum and I had even longer to talk. She was reflecting on what a 'good and exciting life' she and my father had been able to have. I asked her what were the most exciting parts. Of course, she lovingly named her children, their marriages, and her grandchildren. She was especially excited about the first child my wife and I were expecting. She spoke about the work of their church and all their friends. But what was most exciting to her was the mission work they had been able to do since they had retired. She ended up talking about that for at least the next hour.

During the years just before the fall of the Berlin Wall, my parents had volunteered with a missionary group that supported and assisted struggling Christians in several Eastern European countries. Communist regimes were very tough on religious believers, who faced isolation, discrimination and even persecution for their faith. The group my parents joined worked to provide food, medicine, books, Bibles, information, communication and Christian fellowship to the beleaguered Christians, often clandestinely.

As an older retired couple, looking like tourists in their minivan, my parents were the perfect ones to make the runs of contraband into tightly controlled Eastern bloc countries. My parents! I could hardly contain my chuckles over the phone as my mother told me how she and my father would drive into a deserted Bulgarian forest to retrieve the illegal materials from the false panels of a minivan or the fake propane tank in the trunk of a car. My mum told me how my dad would sit in the driver's seat while she would lock herself inside the dark trunk and, with a flashlight, reach inside a fake propane gas tank to pull out dozens of books, papers, rations and computer disks! 'My arms are smaller than his', she explained. Then they would attempt to make contact (with passwords) with Christians they had never met in the massive grey apartment complexes of East European cities – bringing them critical and sustaining materials, hugs and hope. 'It was such a privilege to meet people who have sacrificed so much for their faith', she said. 'Even though we didn't speak the same language, we always found ways to communicate'. Though they had lived long, rich and busy lives, my parents felt these were the most exciting times they ever had.

She knew I could easily understand that. My own pilgrimage had taken me from the inner city of Detroit to urban and rural terrains all across America, to Nicaraguan villages, Filipino barrios, South African townships and Middle East refugee camps. My parents watched as their children, armed with the values they had taught us, ventured out of the house to places they never imagined we would go. Then, when they had the chance, they did it too, in their own way. We were blessed with a wonderful home, but all of us realized that sometimes you've got to get out of the house.

Chapter Three

Use Your Gift

There are varieties of gifts,
but the same Spirit. (1 Corinthians 12.4)

I'M AN OCCASIONAL LISTENER to a very popular National Public Radio
show called *Car Talk*. The call-in programme is ostensibly about
problems with your car, but it's the humour of the two brother
mechanics who co-host the show that keeps most of us tuned in.
When I'm home at the weekend, my Saturday-morning routine
often has me in the shower with *Car Talk* turned up very loud.

On one such Saturday, I was showering, still half asleep, when
I heard one of the *Click and Clack* brothers intone, 'Never criticize
a man until you have walked for a mile in his shoes.' A long
pause followed. Then he continued, 'Because then, when you
criticize him, you will be a mile away...and you'll have his
shoes!' I remember laughing out loud under the shower spray.
They had woken me up. I couldn't believe at first that he was
actually repeating such an old tired slogan. But then he gave it a
little twist, turned it into something funny, unexpected, and even
provocative. They were being creative.

That's what we have to be – creative. When it comes to doing
something about poverty, for example, we've got to move beyond
the old tired slogans. We've got to stop talking about the under-
privileged people who need some help from those of us who are
better off. In the midst of busy lives and schedules, the more
affluent are made to feel guilty enough to write a cheque or
maybe even donate a little time. It's a small price to pay for a clear
conscience. And all we're talking about is donating tins of food or
helping a church or charity with a special Thanksgiving or

Christmas dinner. The more serious ongoing work of dealing with poor people is left to the professionals, perhaps social workers or clergy. Worst of all, many people, while supporting cuts in public programmes and taxes, still expect the government to 'take care of' poor people.

All that needs to change and, thankfully, is beginning to. Consider this dramatic scene.

The Altar Call

The church hall was full of ordinary people from a middle-sized town in the Pacific Northwest. The subject was youth violence, which had become an increasing and frightening reality in the community. Some enterprising pastors and youth workers had assembled a wide collection of young people from the streets, representing gangs from virtually every race and ethnicity in the city, both male and female. The kids were quite a sight, sitting up in the front, being scrutinized by the respectable citizens of the community. Attired in backwards baseball caps, bandannas and baggy trousers, and with their body pierces and tattoos, they told their stories.

The young men and women were reluctant at first, but soon began to share their personal sagas of how they had fallen through the cracks and ended up on the street. The stories were very moving, and as is often the case, the personal and even intimate sharing began to break down the barriers of fear and distrust. The concerned but initially wary citizens began to understand how lost and lonely kids get lured into gangs and into trouble. Slowly they began to see these kids as 'our children' and not just as 'gang members'.

But what happened next was truly remarkable. Somebody asked what they could do. One of the kids said, 'I dunno, man, maybe you could figure out what you do best and just use it.' Before long, I was witnessing something akin to an old-fashioned altar call. A college dean stood up and offered to take these young people on a tour of his campus, and if they were willing to really work hard, he would work on arranging the necessary scholarships. A downtown pastor said he would open up his church after school and at night, when the kids had said they had no safe places to go. A county drug-enforcement officer asked if some of the kids might give him advice about how to be most effective, and a policeman said he would like to get their help too. Several business leaders had jobs they wanted to talk to the young people about. Even the media people who were there said they would like to help get these kids' stories out to the general public.

But my favourite was a middle-aged woman who stood up and said, 'I'm not the dean of any college, the pastor of a church, or the president of a company, but I've got something to offer too. I work at the McDonald's downtown and get a morning and afternoon break. Lots of you kids said you've got nobody to talk to. Well, now you know where to find me, and I'll even buy you a cup of coffee.' I liked her offer the best because she understood an especially important principle: Offering whatever you have and whatever you are is enough. Too many people don't believe that, so they don't get involved. Because we can't do what we think would really make a big difference, we don't offer our own gift – whatever that is.

Unlike many church and charitable organizations today, Jesus taught his disciples not to value the biggest and most important gifts, but rather those that are most sacrificial. One day while Jesus was teaching in the Jewish temple, he sat down opposite the place where people made their offerings and watched the crowd putting money into the treasury. Many rich people put in large sums. Then a poor widow came and put in two small copper coins, which were worth about a penny. He called his disciples and said to them, 'Truly I tell you, this poor widow has put in more than all those who are contributing to the treasury. For all of them have contributed out of their abundance; but she out of her poverty has put in everything she had, all she had to live on' (Mark 12.43–44).

Be Creative

What I was seeing in the Pacific Northwest was not just concern, but *creativity* in action. Finding your own contribution takes creativity and, not surprisingly, your best contribution always comes out of what is most creative for you. Do what you do best, but do it in a way that makes a difference. How could your best gift be applied in new and creative ways to make real social change possible?

Creativity can be risky. Getting out of the house takes some courage, but getting involved will begin to test you. It may change

your view of the world and your perceptions of who you are and
what you can do. You'll learn to assess what you can offer, and
even what you can handle. The important thing is just to start
somewhere. Be creative and find somewhere to make an
investment of time and commitment, and the next steps will
naturally follow. Even if it seems awkward at first, your creative
personal involvement will help show you the way forward.

I talk to business people and bank managers about helping
former gang leaders start micro-enterprise businesses. I hear how
busy professionals build time at a community food bank or
homeless shelter into their family schedules. I listen to successful
editors who look forward to their writing class each week with a
group of urban youths. I've watched doctors set aside lucrative
careers to set up clinics for at-risk kids. There's no substitute for
personal involvement. No matter where you're starting, there is
something you can do that will lead you to what might come
next. People just like you are getting involved in mentoring,
tutoring or a myriad of volunteer efforts, and it is changing their
lives.

Creativity must be applied in broad terms here. Whenever you
really give of yourself, that's creativity in action. When you enjoy
doing something so much you almost lose yourself in it – that's
creativity and that's what will fulfil you. It's what you were made
to be and do, and when you find it, nothing is more satisfying. It's
not just ego to find your best gift; it's acting with creativity and
integrity. Finally, it is acting in faith.

How do we harness that creativity to change our communities
while at the same time fulfilling our souls? To be made in the
image of God is to be creative. And to be fully human is to
connect the image of God in you to that image in others – across
all the dividing lines. Creativity might be more than volunteering
in a soup kitchen, though that is always a good place to start.
Stories of people from all walks of life who are finding their best
contribution show the wide possibilities of creativity.

Some of My Friends

I want to give you examples from people around me – friends,
co-workers, people in many walks of life – who have decided to
be creative with the things that they do best.

My doctor is a woman named Janelle Goetcheus. Janelle was a

successful doctor in the Midwest with a lucrative career. But something kept tugging at her soul. Janelle was feeling compelled to do something more important with her medical skills, something more consistent with her faith. In response to a clear sense of 'call', as Janelle puts it, she and her whole family moved from Ohio to Washington, DC, to join the Church of the Saviour, which, they heard, wanted to begin a medical ministry focused on poor and underserved people in the nation's capital. Dr Goetcheus first opened the Columbia Road Health Services for recent immigrants from Central America, many of them without legal status in the United States. Soon the waiting room was filled with mothers and children who couldn't speak English and had virtually nowhere else to go for medical care.

Shortly after that came Christ House, a medical facility for the homeless sick. Not allowed to stay in most hospitals but too sick to live on the streets, homeless men and women found a safe haven that was compassionate, personal, competent and even cost effective (the cost for a person at Christ House is $47.00 per day, while the cost of the same services in the DC hospital system is almost $700.00). Janelle has helped to establish and staff several other clinics around the city and often can be found in the Health Care for the Homeless van that brings medical services to homeless people on the street who can't or won't go to a clinic. Other spin-offs followed, such as Joseph's House, a place to care for those living with AIDS.

Even beyond the countless numbers of poor people served by her clinics, Dr Janelle Goetcheus has become the medical conscience of Washington, DC. Public health officials, city council budget-cutters, and neglectful federal officials overseeing the District of Columbia have all felt the power of her soft-spoken but persistent advocacy of the health needs and rights of the poorest of the poor. Other doctors, all over the city, have lined up to offer their specializations to treat 'Janelle's patients'. And a new generation of young doctors has been inspired and trained by this woman who heard a call.

When my wife and I needed a doctor for our first pregnancy, Janelle suggested Dr Mark Hathaway, a young man who had just finished his residency. We found him in our local neighbourhood clinic, which treats very low-income people almost exclusively. When I asked this bright young doctor why he chose to work there instead of at a modern hospital, Dr Hathaway replied, 'I really like working with the people here, and I enjoy being a part of their lives.' He also said he had been inspired by Dr Janelle Goetcheus. She's one woman who has been able to make a real difference in health care for the poor throughout an entire city.

Henry Freeman is a fund-raiser, and a very good one. He raised millions of dollars for the University of Michigan as its vice-president for development. But his Quaker social conscience prompted some changes, and soon he was raising millions of dollars for Earlham College, a small Quaker school in Indiana. Then what was happening in Central America began to trouble him. So he joined a group of people taking a trip to El Salvador to find out what was going on. I've described the impact of such journeys before. The trip changed Henry Freeman. More trips to El Salvador pricked his conscience as he met children in rural villages who would never have the chance to go to school. Henry decided to try to change that by doing what he does best – raising money. At the last count, he had successfully put 150 Salvadorean children through school, and the first ones are already graduating from college. Many are now going back to their communities to help make a difference for their families and neighbours.

One day Henry got a packet in the post. In it was a large piece of paper with the fingerprints of many of the children he had put through school. It was their thank-you to this North American man who had made such a difference in their lives. The tears in the savvy fund-raiser's eyes indicated which part of his work was closest to his heart. It wasn't long before Henry was devoting all of his time to consulting on projects that he thought were making a real difference for social justice. *Sojourners* magazine was Henry's first consulting project, and he has really helped us. I've watched how effective a very skilled person can be when he applies his creative best to something he truly believes in.

And speaking of magazines, the story of our art director is another good one. Ed Spivey was surprised when a *Wall Street Journal* staff person told him that he had got the best job straight out of college among all 1971 journalism graduates. Starting as art director for the Chicago *Sun-Times* Sunday magazine was a big job for a kid from Vincennes, Indiana. I met Ed shortly after he moved to Chicago, when he began to attend events where I was speaking and came around to visit the little community we were starting on Chicago's North Side. When our fledgling publication finally needed a real art director, I invited Ed over for dinner, hoping to get some advice and maybe some volunteer time at evenings and weekends. But Ed surprised all of us when he said he was ready to quit his job and join us. I remember hearing that the *Sun-Times* managing editor took Ed out for lunch to try to dissuade him from 'throwing away your career'. But Ed persisted in his new calling, and he's been with *Sojourners* ever since, winning many awards for his designs and layouts.

So many innovative projects are underfunded, especially at first, and really depend on the commitments of people willing to offer their gifts and creativity to the enterprise at below market value. Ed's done work for scores of organizations and projects that he believes in, knowing that a message will get through much more effectively if it is well presented graphically and appeals to the senses as well as the sensibilities. Ed told me he would be embarrassed to be mentioned in the same chapter as people like Janelle Goetcheus because he believes himself to be a very ordinary person who has just learned the skills of graphic design. But that's exactly why he does belong here. The world, or your part of it, will not be changed by a few highly talented professionals turning their successful careers in the direction of community service. Rather, our world will be transformed only when enough ordinary people decide to live by their best values and beliefs.

My favourite social policy analyst is John DiIulio. From an Italian working-class neighbourhood in Philadelphia, John went to Harvard and graduated with a doctorate in political science. He was a tenured professor at Princeton at the age of 28. DiIulio has gone on to become a genuine public intellectual, directing major research centres, writing both popular and academic works on American government, crime and social policy, and regularly contributing to scholarly journals, national magazines and newspaper editorial opinion pages. But in the last few years, DiIulio's Catholic faith kicked in as his analysis of the real crisis facing urban youngsters deepened. He has given himself over to research, writing and civic action on faith-based approaches to urban problems, 'now my life's work', he says. DiIulio wasn't content with a successful career but rather chose to apply his particular gifts to a concrete social project: 'Getting resources to people who are successfully working with the kids, and changing federal, state and local government policies that will directly benefit those kids – that's my bottom line ... that's it!'

DiIulio's support for urban black pastors in Boston, for example, was instrumental in gaining major national media coverage of their very hopeful efforts. Their success in dramatically reducing youth crime drew wide public attention to the promise of faith communities finding solutions to social problems all around the country. As an insider in the think-tank policy world, he has also used his influence with several foundations to secure major funding for efforts that would otherwise have struggled to get the resources they needed. John also volunteers at an inner-city school in Philadelphia, teaching street-level civics to urban kids. He's not only an intellectual but also a man who tries to practise what he preaches.

You have to ask yourself what your goals really are. Do you just want to be successful, respected and secure – perhaps prosperous or even famous – or do you also want to try to make a real difference? What do you most aspire to? Do you want to do something that will make a difference in the lives of people who need it most? 'What are your best skills and gifts going to be used for in this world?' is another way of asking the question.

Those stories from my doctor, my fund-raiser, my art director and my favourite policy analyst make the point. Discover what you do best, then do it in a way that makes a difference.

Sometimes taking the vocational skills you have developed and applying them to volunteer activities is a good way forward. Pulitzer Prize-winning *Washington Post* columnist Mary McGrory, for example, spends time each week teaching children how to read. Often, McGrory says, she just goes in and reads to children in school. All of us are busy, but few are busier than a successful national columnist and commentator. But at the national volunteer summit in Philadelphia, in April 1997, McGrory spoke movingly about the importance of her volunteer activity to the rest of her life and work. It is real, hands-on, practical and personal. Sometimes you see the difference you are making; other times you learn how deep and complex the problems really are. But either way, you feel involved.

At our neighbourhood centre, we try to link every child or young person with adult mentors and role models who will help them find *their* creative gift. A group of young people will work with a poet on learning how to write poetry; the centre has already published several wonderful volumes of poetry from the kids. If a young person thinks he or she might want to be an architect, we find an architect to serve as a mentor. Linda DeGraf, a local artist and teacher, helped the children to create their own mural, depicting the positive and hopeful things about our neighbourhood. At first, the kids were convinced they couldn't do it – only real artists could do something like that. But she patiently showed them how to discover their potential. To their great surprise, the new young artists succeeded in producing a beautiful work of neighbourhood art, a picture of which appeared on the front page of the *Washington Post's* District Weekly section.

Churches Can Be Creative Too

When the welfare Bill was passed in the autumn of 1996, it sent everyone scrambling in states and communities around the country. The new law didn't really reform welfare; it just ended the old system – without any alternatives in place. Ever since, many people – from elected officials to service providers to local pastors – have been trying to figure out what to do. In the spring of 1997, I was invited to North Carolina to speak to pastors and lay church leaders on that subject. After relating the biblical imperatives to fight for poor families, I challenged the North Carolina churches to step forward. Be the leader here, I urged. Somebody has got to lead the way to make welfare reform really work. Someone has to show our society how to help families move out of poverty. The churches can't do it by themselves, I said, but they could play the leadership role as a catalyst, a convener and a venue for finding some new solutions and building some new partnerships.

A year later, I was asked back. 'We've been doing it,' I was told by Diana Jones Wilson, the whirlwind of an organizer who invited me in the first place, 'now it's time to talk about next steps.' What I found in North Carolina was truly amazing. The churches had trained more than 5,000 people to become involved in welfare-to-work efforts. Pastors were directly involved in the training, along with lay church members from all walks of life. Together they made plans for supporting people in the difficult journey from welfare and poverty to work and community. The churches were also taking a leading role in education and advocacy for state policy changes that would make a real difference to low-income people. In some counties, church members were now leading the state's welfare-to-work programme. One day Diana called me. Her voice was calm, but I could tell she was excited about something. 'I wanted to tell you what has happened as a result of the work we've done since you came two years ago,' she said. She reported that the churches of North Carolina had just received a grant of $1.25 million from their state to support and expand their leadership in welfare reform.

In Raleigh, North Carolina, one of the most creative new programmes has sprung up. The Jobs Partnership in Raleigh has organized 100 churches to mentor former welfare recipients through a 12-week training course that uses Bible study to teach workplace skills. In two years, 300 programme graduates have found jobs, and 95 per cent still work for the first company that hired them. As the programme director, the Revd Skip Long, says, 'All we've done is help them dream again.'

Riverside Church on New York City's Upper West Side has a long and distinguished history of social concern and action. For years it has implemented extensive social service programmes from its massive Gothic structure next to the Hudson River. But when the welfare Bill of 1996 was passed, the church mobilized as never before. Under the leadership of its pastor, Dr James Forbes, employers in the church began to provide jobs, volunteers helped prepare welfare recipients to get and keep work, groups organized to surround poor families with the support they needed to make the difficult transition, and many people got into the act of job training and preparedness. Jim Forbes's barber trained 30 welfare recipients to become barbers themselves! Almost any church, even those much smaller than Riverside, has lots of people with skills and creativity to share. It just has to be mobilized.

People from almost every kind of work in the country are finding creative ways to shape their vocation in the direction of service and justice. It is possible. If nothing else, it is the children who cry out for our personal involvement. It's their vulnerability that calls us to start by doing something, not our own sense of readiness. Rabbi Hillel sums up our call to action well: 'If I am not for myself, who will be? If I am only for myself, what am I? If not now, when?'

How to Slay a Giant

Community organizer Marshall Ganz tells a wonderful story from the biblical book of 1 Samuel, the story of David and Goliath. He uses this famous episode to illustrate the point I've been making about using your gift. Ganz recounts: 'As you recall, Goliath comes forth from the Philistines to do battle with the Israelites. He is big, he is powerful, and he is a veteran of many wars. The Israelite soldiers are frightened. No one will volunteer to face him. At this point, David, a young shepherd, steps forth. "I'll do it," he says. The men laugh at him. He's but a shepherd, and a boy at that. But the spirit of the Lord has come into him. And pay attention to this. He doesn't know *how* he's going to do it before he volunteers to do it – no strategic plan for David.

'Well, he goes to see King Saul and King Saul laughs at him too. "You're but a shepherd, but a boy." "Yes," admits David, "but I want to fight, I'm willing to fight, and no one else will do it anyway." "Well, all right," agrees the king, "but Goliath is an experienced warrior. Take my sword, my shield, and my helmet. Put these on. You'll need them to protect you." Excited that he's been given the opportunity to fight, David puts them on, but as he gets them on he starts to feel uncomfortable. "Wait a minute," he thinks. "I don't know how to use these things, I've 'proved them not'." At that moment he glances at the small stream that is flowing by his feet and he sees five smooth stones there. And as he looks at the stones, he remembers, "I'm not a warrior, but I am a shepherd. And as a shepherd I know how to protect my flock from the wolf and the lion – and it was with stones and a sling, not a sword and a shield. Maybe Goliath is just another wolf." Well, you know the rest. He takes off the armour, picks up the stones, and, using his sling, defeats the mighty Goliath, surprised that a young shepherd boy should be the source of his undoing.'

Ganz then reflects, 'So what does this story teach us about strategy? Well, David comes up with a way in which resourcefulness makes up for what looked like a lack of resources. First of all, he doesn't have it all figured out before he acts. It's his commitment to act that puts him in a position where he really has to use his intelligence to figure out how to do it – he's motivated. What else? Where does he look for the answer? He considers using the tools of his powerful opponent to defeat him but thinks better of it. No, he reflects on his own experience, his own resources, and his own skills to find a means of defeating Goliath. And he finds the means when he recontextualizes the arena in which he finds himself – seeing it no longer as field of battle on which two soldiers will face each other, but as a pasture in which a shepherd confronts a wolf. He was an outsider to the battle. And as an outsider he saw resources others did not see, opportunities others did not see, and so devised a strategy which others did not devise – to Goliath's great surprise. Let us all learn to be David. Let us be faithful enough to trust our own spirit where others do not trust theirs, wise enough to draw on our own experience to see where others do not see, and courageous enough to act on what we do see where others cannot act.'

David was a shepherd who knew how to protect sheep, and he defeated the feared Goliath by remembering who he was and using his own gifts. We are always tempted to defer to other people's experience and perspective instead of trusting our own. Instead, we need to find the courage to act upon what we see, not what others do.

Anyone Can Do This

One of the more interesting speaking requests I received recently was an invitation from inmates at the Sing Sing prison, just north of New York City. An innovative programme at Sing Sing, run by the New York Theological Seminary, provides theological training behind the prison walls and is the only effort of its kind in the country. In a very rigorous course of study, the inmates examine theology, church history and biblical studies in preparation for future ministry both inside and outside of prison. Many of these students also teach their fellow inmates in Sing Sing's college-equivalency programme, there being no one else willing to do it after the federally sponsored college programmes for prison inmates were cut, despite their enormously successful track record.

Students from both programmes had studied my book *The Soul of Politics* and now were inviting the author to come and talk with them about it. When we asked about scheduling, they replied that they were a relatively 'captive' audience and were 'free' most nights of the week.

It was well worth the trip. Seventy men crowded into the room, and our discussion went on for three hours. Its intensity rivalled anything I had ever experienced at Harvard or other universities. More than three years after the book had been written, they knew it better than I did. We scrutinized idea after idea, concept after concept, always asking how it might be applied on the street. Their clear motivation was to go back to the street, back to the community, with what they had learned. They were determined to influence young men to make different choices than they had. These inmates had, in fact, become experts in many of the social problems that plague our communities. They knew the realities firsthand and talked movingly about their lives and their experience.

Some knew they would never leave prison but had decided to dedicate themselves to ministering to fellow prisoners, helping their brothers turn their lives around. But others longed for the day when they would go home. Instead of escaping the realities from which they had come, most wanted to return to those places in order to change them. Most of the prisoners at Sing Sing, the inmates told me, have come from only about four New York City neighbourhoods, in the poorest parts of the city. One man spoke movingly about 'the train' that leaves from neighbourhoods like his, loading on boys as young as nine or ten, and heading for the eventual destination of Sing Sing. How do we stop that train, he asked.

I was impressed. There were no doctors, bankers or politicians here. These were almost entirely men who had started near the bottom of their society and ended up in prison, the very bottom. To succumb to bitterness, cynicism, or hopelessness here is very easy. Yet these men hadn't. Instead they had decided to take their gift – their experience – and use it to help change younger men's lives before it was too late. That's not only creative, it's courageous – two strengths our society desperately needs.

One of the Sing Sing theologians made a comment that stayed with me long after I left the prison yard. He was sharing his experiences of poverty, crime and prison. He said he had clearly been on a downward spiral going nowhere. But then 'a light came on', and he could see the trajectory of his life and where it was heading. That was when he decided to change his direction. Many of us are on a trajectory with our lives going nowhere good. We may not be heading to prison, except prisons of our own making. But we may also be missing a life direction that could result in accomplishments of lasting value or fulfil the deepest longings of our souls. We too need a light to come on.

We need many lights to come on if we are to overcome the poverty that grips our nation's soul. That will happen when all of us have the courage and the creativity to find our own best contribution. And as our brothers at Sing Sing remind us, it is never too late to find our gift.

Chapter Four

Do the Work and You'll Find the Spirit

If you offer your food to the hungry and satisfy the needs of the afflicted, then your light shall rise in the darkness and your gloom be like the noonday. (Isaiah 58.10)

SPIRITUAL RENEWAL will supply the energy for justice. Faith and spirituality could become the most powerful forces for social justice in the beginning of a new millennium. That would seem, to many, a bold and even unbelievable statement, given the common perceptions of religion today and the inward preoccupation of so much contemporary spirituality. During much of the twentieth century, religion was regarded as a mostly private affair and, at its worst, was a reactionary influence. With the great exception of the black churches, religion in twentieth-century America was not a great force for justice. Likewise, much of the resurgence of spirituality we've seen over the last several years has been successfully commercialized into mere self-help. Nonetheless, many factors now point to the probability that spirituality and faith will return to the dynamic social role they have often played before. The spiritual power of faith to change history is being rediscovered.

I believe in the linkage of faith and justice in part because of my own story, which I told in Chapter 1. Now, as a new millennium has begun, many religious people are being drawn into the struggle for social change, having seen and felt the limits of purely private religion. At the same time, many people outside of religion are hungry for the power and promise of spirituality.

Social movements need a combination of spirituality and practical goals. That's a lesson I've learned over many years. The civil rights movement evidenced a powerful spirituality. But it also held out the promise of freedom for black Americans, a tremendous motivating force. And it promised white allies the possibility of healing an uneasy conscience and fulfilling the ideals of the American dream. Dr King used to say that he held his Bible in one hand and the American Constitution in the other. The most successful movements must offer people the chance to better their lives and fulfil their deepest moral convictions and aspirations.

Robert Putnam, in a much discussed article entitled 'Bowling Alone', set off alarms about declining civic participation in American life. I participated in a three-year discussion, led by Putnam, which focused on how to rekindle civic engagement in America today. A very diverse group of scholars, journalists, elected officials, business people, artists, pastors, political analysts and grassroots activists examined many areas of American life, searching for the things that create 'social capital'. One conclusion many of us drew from the Saguaro Seminar was that it takes more than activities to create positive social engagement; it requires a spirituality of social responsibility, by which I mean a reason for action that transcends ourselves. We can simply be critical of all the individualism and self-help energy in the Western world that focuses so much on ourselves, or we can try to link the desire for personal fulfilment with social responsibility by drawing on the ancient wisdom of Isaiah, which, as I'll explain, provides a powerful spirituality for social engagement.

Isaiah's wisdom suggests that it is really impossible to separate the desire for personal growth from the call for social responsibility. You may succeed in getting physically fit, but your 10 km run may take you past so many homeless people that you can't keep averting your eyes. If you achieve financial success, you'll discover that pollution, violence and cultural decay don't stop at your carefully wired door alarms and security fences. Meditation may give you peace of mind, but it won't protect your family from unforeseen possibilities, like corporate downsizing. And your quality of life can be dramatically affected by social problems such as youth crime, racial hostility, economic dislocation and the collapse of cultural values, or by overseas conflicts that don't get resolved by peaceful means.

No matter how much we try to love and guard our children, we can't ultimately shield them from what's going on all around them. If we are fortunate enough to raise our kids well, how will they react to kids who never had a 'safe, fair, healthy, or moral start', to quote the priorities of Marian Wright Edelman's Children's Defense

Fund? How do we explain to our children why people of different skin colours often don't live in the same neighbourhoods or worship together in America? What if our kids ask us about the third world children whose exploited labour makes our family's clothes and prevents them from playing as our children do? And even if we manage to prepare for our children's education, foreign policy can send our young sons and daughters off to a dangerous war zone.

The health and well-being of our souls is of utmost importance. Can they ever be independent of the health of the world or the well-being of our neighbour? All our religious traditions say they cannot. Spiritual principles teach us that the best things we do for others are also the best things we do for ourselves, and that we are connected to one another whether we like it or not. Real security, faith reminds us, is found through widening and deepening our circle of community, rather than finding our own individual solutions.

Young people are discovering this wisdom. Frequently I speak on college campuses and find students signing up for service projects in unprecedented numbers. As I travel across the country, I find middle-class young people volunteering much more time than is needed to balance their CVs. Thousands of students are venturing beyond campus walls to spend hours each week with poor children, are giving up beer-drinking vacations in the sun to do work projects on their spring breaks, and are taking a year or two after college to plunge into tough urban neighbourhoods and daunting overseas programmes.

Isaiah's Wisdom: Connection and Meaning

I ask students why they are doing these things, frequently at genuine sacrifice and even real risk to themselves. It's sometimes hard for them to put their answers into words, but they always end up saying that the time they spend with an inner-city kid or working with a poor family on their new house makes *them* feel so much better – they feel better about their lives, their faith, their future and their world. The most common words I hear are 'connection' and 'meaning'. They talk about the connection they feel to people they hadn't felt connected to before. The connection brings healing and gives their life a sense of meaning and purpose.

The biblical prophet Isaiah understood this many centuries ago. In the Book of Isaiah, Chapter 58, the prophet describes what the Lord requires 'to loose the bonds of injustice, to undo the thongs of the yoke, to let the oppressed go free, and to break every yoke'. The prophet's call for direct personal involvement is as contemporary as if it were written yesterday: 'Is it not to share your bread with the hungry, and bring the homeless poor into your house; when you see the naked, to cover them, and not to hide yourself from your own kin?

'Then your light shall break forth like the dawn, and *your* healing shall spring up quickly' (my italics). *Your* healing is at stake here, says Isaiah, not just *theirs* – the poor. Isaiah made a profound point that is often lost in self-help America today: the path to genuine healing and self-fulfilment is the journey that connects us to other people, and especially to poor and marginalized people.

Conventional wisdom expresses exactly the opposite. How often have you heard people say something like this: 'I would like to get involved in some kind of service, but first I have to get my own life together.' Isaiah is saying (and the college students are finding) that the best way to get your life together is to do something for somebody else – then will your light 'break forth' and your own healing 'spring up quickly.' In fact, to focus only upon yourself and your own needs could prove to be a great obstacle to real satisfaction.

In other words, if you just work on getting your own life together you may never succeed in doing so. There are always enough things going on in our lives to absorb all of our attention and time. That may be the very trap that prevents us from really getting our lives in order. Contrary to what self-help logic implies, it is only the personal commitment to move beyond ourselves and the narrow confines of our own little worlds that can bring us the human fulfilment for which we hunger.

Isaiah's description of such human fulfilment is enough to excite the appetite of any self-help enthusiast: 'If you offer your food to the hungry and satisfy the needs of the afflicted, then your light shall rise in the darkness and your gloom be like the noonday. The Lord will guide you continually, and satisfy your needs in parched places, and make your bones strong; and you shall be like a watered garden, like a spring of water, whose waters never fail. Your ancient ruins shall be rebuilt; you shall raise up the foundations of many generations; you shall be called the repairer of the breach, the restorer of streets to live in.'

Isaiah's image of both personal and social healing is one of the most powerful in all spiritual literature. The connection between the two is crucial. Here is the bridge between self-help and social action so many in our society are looking to find. The link between personal growth and social responsibility is a spiritual one. How we long to be nurtured like a watered garden or to have our streets restored as good and safe places. And Isaiah was speaking to a people, not just to individuals. 'If' you do these things, says Isaiah, 'then' you will reap this harvest of healing. If you act in justice, you will know the healing that comes from reconnection. But you can't have one without the other.

It's inspiring to see what happens at our neighbourhood centre between an eight-year-old girl and a 19-year-old college student from nearby Howard University who is helping her work on reading. The youngster thinks, 'She's a black woman, just like I am going to be. She's smart and she's in college. She likes me, I can tell. And she thinks I'm smart, too. She thinks I could go to college. Maybe I will!' In the meantime, the Howard student is watching that child and thinking to herself, 'This kid is changing my life. The best two hours of my week are the time I spend with her. That's when I feel like I'm making some difference in the world and my own life means something. We're making a connection here. I can't go back to my studies and career track to money and success as if nothing has happened to me. I want to do something with my life that makes a difference in the lives of kids like her!' That is what Isaiah is talking about.

It is not someone doing something 'for' someone else. That's key. There's a relationship here that is changing *both* people. This crucial dynamic of transformation must be expanded to the broadest level if real social change is going to occur. But this isn't just limited to students and young people. The key is getting people of all ages and from all sectors of society involved in offering their best gifts where they are most needed.

I remember one Sunday morning, preaching at Rising Hope Church, newly founded by Keary Kincannon, a former member of our Sojourners Community. He had become a Methodist pastor and had started a new congregation in Virginia, mostly for low-income people. They hold a wonderful service – friendly, warm

and open enough to attract poor people, among them several
homeless people. I preached from the text of Isaiah 58, about how
reaching out to others can help to heal your own soul. In the
discussion time that always follows the sermon at Rising Hope, a
member of the congregation shot his hand up and testified, 'That's
exactly what happened to me!'

His name was Chuck, and he proceeded to tell his story. 'After
my wife died, I got very depressed. I missed her so much, and life
just didn't seem very good to me any more. But I was coming to
church, and that's when I met Wanda over there. She was homeless
then and didn't have anywhere to live. I had space and decided I
could take her in. Now I'm too busy to be depressed any more! It's
really working well.'

All alone with no money or job, Wanda was living in shelters.
But one day in church, a kindly older man said he had a spare
room if she needed it. Chuck's house became a place to stay while
Wanda got her life together. And that's exactly what she was now
doing. 'If you take the homeless into your house,' said Chuck,
paraphrasing Isaiah, 'then you'll get healed!' Isaiah was right,
Chuck testified. 'That's just what happened to me!'

Pursuing the common good *is* essential to our individual well-
being. Healthy communities *are* critical to healthy families. The
surrounding cultural values *do* have a major impact on the
personal choices of our children. The quality of our political
debate can serve or destroy the integrity of the public square,
which affects our private lives in all kinds of ways. In all these
things, the public and private are deeply connected. Breakdowns
in families and communities will affect the larger body politic and,
conversely, when the body politic is ill, the virus can infect us all.
Human society is like a great piece of fabric; when the unravelling
begins in one part of it, the tear threatens to undo the whole
cloth.

Isaiah speaks to the point when he challenges those who simply
engage in 'the pointing of the finger, the speaking of evil'. Rather,
he says, 'offer your food to the hungry, and satisfy the needs of the
afflicted.' In other words, stop all your blaming and posturing and
instead do something concrete to make a difference and do some
good. Isaiah directly enters the political arena when speaking of
'repairing the breach' and 'restoring of streets to dwell in'. He
directly poses the challenge of seeking the common good over
partisan self-interest.

Are there not lessons to be learned in cooling youth violence, reducing teen pregnancy, overcoming addictions, ending homelessness, giving children a good start, helping welfare recipients succeed in work, or creating more equitable institutions? I think there are. But it all comes back to Isaiah's vital connection between personal well-being and social justice.

Islands of Hope

Those who say the world cannot be changed are mistaken. At a dinner I attended with several former members of Congress, governors and mayors, a statement was made: 'Nobody has answers any more in America.' I disagreed. I invited the politicians to name the social problems they were most concerned about, and then gave them the names of people and projects that are finding solutions to each one (sometimes naming efforts in their own states and cities). They were amazed to learn that answers to some of our most difficult problems are already out there.

I suggested these efforts were like islands in a vast and threatening sea. If you can swim to an island, you will probably be all right. But if you can't get there, or don't even know in which direction to swim, you will be in real trouble. Today, our islands are still too few and far between, but they are out there. Our task must be to connect the islands, create the resources to greatly expand their territory and, finally, take what we can learn from the islands to forge new social policy. But first, we have to get the word out that changing our communities is *not* an impossible task.

How do we change the world, or at least our corner of it? That's the big question, isn't it? Sure, we can all improve ourselves; literally thousands of books have been written to help us succeed in changing our individual lives. But changing the world, by starting with where we live – now that's a different story.

I don't mean changing everything, especially all at once, or in a way that will last for ever. No, we don't need any more utopian visions. Those have led to some of our worst problems. But we do need change, and most of us feel it. We need change in our neighbourhoods, our schools, our congregations, our workplaces, our cities, our country and, certainly, around our world. We don't need things to be perfect (they never will be); we do need a world that's more fair, more safe, more honest and more just.

I'm appealing to the growing moral energy in the country for service, both in individuals and in families. And I'm especially hoping to engage a whole generation of young people, who are searching for meaning and connection.

The time is ripe to build a new spiritual movement for and with poor people. But such a movement must make the Isaiah connection between personal renewal and social change. If you do the work, you'll find the spirit.

Chapter Five

Recognize the Three Faces of Poverty

Blessed are you who are poor. (Luke 6.20)
One does not live by bread alone. (Matthew 4.4)
Then you will know the truth and the truth will make you free.
(John 8.32)

I'VE BEEN WORKING to overcome poverty for three decades now and have learned some things about it along the way. The first is that we still don't understand poverty very well. Many middle-class people seem to want to underestimate or minimize the problem of *material poverty*. Or we want to blame poor people themselves for their predicament. The systemic causes of poverty and the moral indifference of the affluent are not popular subjects in mainstream society. But at a deeper level, a materialistic society fails to recognize its own *spiritual poverty*. The fact that all our anxious striving has impoverished the soul of America is a spiritual reality that we are still not quite ready to face; yet, at some deep level, most of us know it is true. One of the ways I've changed is that I now take our spiritual poverty much more seriously than I used to. In battling to get the richest nation on earth to address its own widespread poverty and the appalling gaps between our lifestyle and that of much of the rest of the world, I often underestimated the spiritual consequences of the nervous and shallow existence so many people in the West find themselves trapped in. I've also begun to see how our political life suffers from a deep and growing spiritual and moral impoverishment. The widespread cynicism, the alarming levels of political withdrawal, the increasing control by moneyed elites and the coarsening of our public debate can best be understood as a kind of *civic poverty*.

Isaiah's wisdom, which we have just discussed, actually addresses all three faces of poverty. In making the connection between personal and social healing, the prophet suggests that there is more to poverty than just economics. And there is a strategy here. Reach out to the members of your community who are poor or forgotten, and you will find satisfaction for your soul and health for your society.

Isaiah is not alone. All our religious and spiritual traditions focus on how we treat materially poor and excluded people, and suggest that the state of poor people is a moral test for the health of any society. And those traditions point us beyond mere charity as a response, calling us more prophetically to the deeper solutions of social and economic justice.

Yet those same traditions also draw our attention to spiritual poverty, which can be experienced among people of any economic status and in fact is often concentrated among the more affluent who have allowed their attachment to things to become a kind of worship in itself. The result is lives without a deep sense of meaning or purpose – lives that feel empty.

And I have come to believe that the breakdown in our public life can also be understood as a form of poverty – civic poverty. The rapid decline of genuine citizen participation and meaningful political discourse is not just a problem for politics, but a moral and spiritual threat to the very essence of democracy.

So we must recognize the three faces of poverty. Recognizing all three poverties and their relatedness is key to overcoming them.

A Climate of Denial

It has become fashionable today to ignore the existence of poverty – or even to deny it. The overgeneralized assumption that we are in the midst of good economic times is consistently used as an excuse to underestimate poverty. And despite the wisdom of Isaiah, our connection to poor people grows more distant.

In 1962, *The Other America*, by Michael Harrington, woke up post-1950s America to the existence of widespread deprivation in the world's wealthiest nation and was credited with sparking President Lyndon Johnson's War on Poverty programme. While real gains were made in those early years and the decades that followed, the war on poverty was never won. And as the effectiveness of government social programmes has come under increasing scrutiny in more recent years, the need to find solutions to the nation's persistent poverty has fallen off the political agenda. Republicans offer a legislative plan of lowering taxes and expanding individual freedom, while Democrats offer a list of programmes to enhance the quality of life for the middle-class, mostly suburban voters, who turn out on election day. Aiming either at the stockbrokers or the soccer mums, neither political party has talked about poor and left-out people for a very long time.

Instead of challenging old approaches and finding new strategies for overcoming poverty, many consider it intellectually and morally respectable to say 'the other America' doesn't exist any more. The problems of tens of millions of people below the poverty line are just explained away. They go on and off welfare; they get lots of other benefits; there are plenty of jobs out there for those who want them; people who are poor usually have other problems besides poverty; economic disadvantage is caused by failures in people's behaviour, not in their society. We've all heard and perhaps even believed some of these sensible-sounding half-truths. This widespread social attitude claims, 'Sure, there are some poor people, but nothing can be done about that, and it's probably their own fault anyway.' But such half-truths are used to avoid facing the whole truth.

Even ten years ago, you could not have got away with denying poverty. The change in climate came in the mid-1990s with the rise of both political conservatism and a booming economy. Some conservative moralists have been trying hard to associate poverty with a lack of virtue as its primary cause, despite the fact that the Bible says the exact opposite – that in a society with widespread poverty, it is the virtue of the rich that is suspect. In the popular culture, individual liberty is in, while the common good is out. Self-help, not social concern, is what fills the magazines and bookshops, and a myriad of commercial offerings are supplied to improve our own quality of life.

The Biblical Argument

The biblical argument flies in the face of this climate of denial. My own moment of real awakening on the question of poor people came in theological seminary. Several of my fellow students and I made a study of every mention of the poor in the Bible. We found several thousand verses on the subject. In the Hebrew Scriptures, it was the second most prominent theme, idolatry being the first, and the two were often related. In the New Testament, one out of

16 verses had to do with wealth and poverty. In the first three Gospels, the subject is in one out of every ten verses; in the Gospel of Luke, it is in one out of seven verses. We were utterly amazed! We became even more incredulous as we discussed our findings and realized that none of us had ever heard a sermon at any of our churches on the danger of riches and God's concern for the poor! Yet the Scriptures were filled with this theme from beginning to end. Why the silence?

That seminary experience gave me one of my most tried and true sermon illustrations. One of my seminary colleagues had taken a pair of scissors to an old Bible, and he proceeded to cut out every single reference to riches or the poor. It took him a very long time. When he finally was finished, the Prophets were decimated, the Psalms destroyed, the Gospels ripped to shreds, and the Epistles turned to tattered rags. The Bible was full of holes. He still has that old torn-up Bible; he's kept it all these years. I used to take it out with me to preach. I'd hold it high above church congregations and say, 'Brothers and sisters, this is our American Bible! It's full of holes!'

The clarity of the Bible on the subject of wealth and poverty seldom comes up in America. You can imagine my surprise when I opened up the *Washington Post* one day and found an editorial opinion piece entitled 'Woe to You Who Are Rich'. Fascinated, I quickly read the opening paragraph, which began, 'Assume that you had never read the New Testament and were given a quiz with the following question: "During His ministry, Christ spoke out most often about (a) the evils of homosexuality, (b) the merits of democracy, (c) family-friendly tax cuts or (d) the danger of riches." It turns out that Christ said nothing about the first three and a lot about the last one. But you'd never know it based on the rhetoric of many modern-day Christians – particularly politically active ones.' The article was by Peter Wehner, the policy director of Empower America, a conservative Republican organization. Wehner pointed out that the Bible is very clear on the issues of wealth and poverty. The article went on to quote large portions of Scripture to show how spiritually dangerous wealth is, according to Jesus and all the biblical writers, and how insistent the Scriptures are in demanding compassion and justice for the poor and oppressed. The clear implication was that America's affluence puts the nation in great spiritual danger, and our lack of concern for the poor is a sign of our moral failing.

US Congressman Tony Hall has counted over 2,500 biblical verses of direct teaching on the subjects of hunger and poverty, a fact that he shared with us at a preach-in for the poor that Call to Renewal held in the US Congress in the wake of the welfare cuts. Hall, a Democrat from Ohio, had just returned from the Sudan and was exhausted from his 41-hour journey but nonetheless wanted to tell us what he had just seen. The congressman spoke quietly and movingly about his time in the Sudan, where he saw hundreds of women and children starving to death. This soft-spoken Christian layman apologized for not being a great preacher like those gathered that day; he went on to say, 'When I see a situation like that, there are a couple of Scriptures that really mean something to me.'

He reached inside his jacket pocket, pulled out a small Bible, and quietly read from Proverbs 14.31: 'He who oppresses the poor shows contempt for their Maker, but whoever is kind to the needy honours God.' Congressman Hall went on, 'We do something for God by being with the poor, preaching for the poor, legislating for the poor. The most important thing I do in Congress is to do the best I can for poor people.' I had never heard so much powerful preaching in a single day before, but the most striking moment of the preach-in came when this sorrowful and tired congressman reported that people were dying needlessly because we didn't care and reminded us that God does.

In the present climate, we may well need to make that kind of religious or spiritual argument against poverty. The self-interest argument alone may not be enough. For years, liberals argued that an investment in the poor is in our own self-interest and good for the economy, at least in the long run. But the booming economy hardly needs those at the bottom any more. And if we just build more prisons, privatize them, and make them profitable by turning the inmate population into a virtual slave-labour force to service the bottom rungs of the economy (to clean our schools and offices at night), we may finally have found a solution for what to do with poor people. It may sound chilling, but that's close to what's happening now. With prison construction and the security industry as two of our fastest-growing economic sectors, the affluent will be well buffered against any contact with poor people, and the current political ethic will make it easier and easier to ignore them.

Clearly we need a theology of solidarity that will bring us together, as Isaiah was calling for. Somehow, the well-being of the poor must be seen to be key to a society's health and welfare. Connecting with one another must be seen as essential for the sake of our own souls. It must never be a matter of guilt, because guilt is a motivation with little staying power. It must become a matter of our mutual well-being, and even our healing. For the poorest among us, the issues are those of survival. For the middle, it's the fear, alienation and loss of human values in a market-driven culture. Many people today fear economic failure and at the same time find economic success increasingly meaningless. As for our society, we see a culture about to give up on finding solutions to any of these problems.

We have to start by understanding poverty better. I've said we have to recognize that poverty has at least three faces. Let's look at each one.

Material Poverty

The first great poverty is *material*. It's what we normally think of when we hear the word 'poverty'. But we still don't understand it very well.

Perhaps the worst thing about material poverty is the exclusion and isolation of those who experience it. There has been so much attention paid these days to what is happening at the top of the economic order that it's easy to forget there is still a very real bottom end. At the bottom, far too many of our fellow citizens are simply excluded from the mainstream of American life, almost untouched by the booming economy. Among those at the bottom are almost *one in six* of our children, who never chose to be born on the outside.

My sister and brother-in-law live around the corner from me in the inner city of Washington, DC. Barb and Jim Tamialis have a wonderful habit of adopting children who need a home. The latest addition to our family is my nephew Marquis, who was one of the district's countless street children. Marquis, whose mother was a crack addict and whose father was nowhere to be found, spent the first decade of his life living in nine different situations. When he became friends with my nine-year-old niece Anika, his mother was in the DC jail. The two kids quickly became best neighbourhood friends, but when Marquis's 75-year-old foster mother from across the street had a stroke, it looked as if he would have to move again. Anika got very sad, and when Anika gets sad, we get mobilized.

Surveying Marquis's limited options, Barb and Jim decided to add him to their family, as they had earlier done with Anika. Everyone was thrilled, especially Marquis.

On one of the first days in his new home, Marquis was in the laundry room chatting with Julie Polter, who lives in the upstairs flat, while she did her wash. 'How long are you going to be here?' Marquis asked. 'Well, I suppose until I finish my laundry,' Julie said, smiling. 'How long are you going to be here?' she playfully replied. Beaming from ear to ear, the new ten-year-old household member asserted confidently, 'I will be staying for ten thousand years!'

For millions of children like Marquis, the most basic provisions of safety, security, shelter, food, education, nurture, love, care and, especially, any hope for the future simply cannot be assumed. All poor children have been left out and left behind. And their numbers are growing. Urban demographers and criminologists predict that a critical mass of such children will reach their adolescent years with virtually no stake in their society.

Marginalized people of all ages are the most vulnerable of God's children. They are, indeed, the focus of religious concern in the Torah, the New Testament and the Koran. It is always the treatment of 'the other' that is the test of faith. But why is that? Why are our religious traditions so strong in commanding us to care for the widow, the orphan, the stranger, the forgotten and the poor? The weak, vulnerable and excluded become the standard for what the rest of society really means by 'community'. Who is part of the family and who is not? Who's in and who's out? Who is 'us' and who is 'them'? Who finally gets to be included in our circle of concern?

Let's put this question another way. Do we regard poor people as citizens or don't we? And if our poorest children are also citizens, what obligations do we have toward them? One thing is now clear: When people are excluded, there will always be consequences – both practically and spiritually. The fundamental questions before us as a society are, simply: Will we include the people in the bottom 25 per cent, and, more profoundly, how can including them help to bring all of us closer together?

The Widening Gap

Increasingly, our economic system is producing a society of extremes. Despite a record-breaking economy, the gap continues to grow between the top and bottom of our society. Virtually no one disputes that any more. Even *Wall Street Journal* articles now agree with the familiar adage 'The rich get richer and the poor get poorer'. The people at the top have received the lion's share of the economic windfall from the economic boom; the middle, far less; and the bottom, almost none at all.

Between 1945 and 1975, the great majority of Americans experienced real and measurable economic progress. The real income of average households doubled, and the percentage of Americans who are poor fell by 60 per cent. During that period, inequality in income and wealth remained constant and even shrank a bit. Overall, the economy grew at rates better than we have experienced these last 20 years. The nation experienced prosperity, but it was much more shared than it is today. It used to be that a rising tide lifted all boats, but the current rising tide is lifting all yachts!

This growing discrepancy means a huge difference in financial security. In the United States, the top 5 per cent of the population now control approximately 60 per cent of the wealth, and the bottom 40 per cent controls just 0.5 per cent. And the top 1 per cent of the population possess a whopping 40 per cent of all American wealth. Since the mid-1970s, the top 1 per cent of households have doubled their share of the national wealth. Never have we seen such a radical redistribution of wealth from the bottom and the middle of society to the top.

Globally, the picture is even starker. In the last five years the number of the world's very poorest people – those who live on less than one dollar per day – has grown 50 per cent, from 1 billion to 1.5 billion. According to the 1998 United Nations Human Development Report, the three richest *people* in the world own assets that exceed the combined gross domestic products of the world's poorest 48 *countries*. Here are some other rather amazing facts from the same report: the world consumed more than $24 trillion in goods and services in 1997, six times the figure for 1995. Of the world's 6.8 billion people, 4.4 billion live in developing (i.e. poor) countries, the rest in transitional or rich industrial countries. Among the 4.4 billion people who live in the poorest countries, three-fifths have no access to basic sanitation, almost one-third are without safe drinking water, one-quarter lack adequate housing, one-fifth live beyond the reach of modern health services, one-fifth of the children do not get as far as grade five in school and one-fifth are undernourished. The report estimates that basic education for all would cost $6 billion a year – while $8 billion is spent annually on cosmetics in the United States alone. Installation of water and basic sanitation for all would cost $9 billion – $11 billion is spent annually on ice cream in Europe. Basic health care and nutrition would cost $13 billion – $17 billion a year is spent on pet food in Europe and the United States. Thirty-five billion dollars is spent on business entertainment in Japan, $50 billion on cigarettes in Europe, $105 billion on alcoholic drinks in Europe, $400 billion on narcotic drugs around the world and $780 billion on the world's armed forces.

The 1997 United Nations Development Programme Report claimed that poverty could be conquered worldwide in the next decade. The cost would be around $80 billion a year until the year 2007 – which is less than one-half of 1 per cent of global income and less than the combined net worth of the seven richest men in the world.

These are, of course, dangerous economic realities but, at a deeper level, they are profoundly moral and even religious issues. The biblical prophets consistently railed against such gross extremes.

When the biblical archaeologists dig down into the ruins of ancient Israel, they find there were periods when the houses were more or less the same size, and the artefacts of life they unearth show there was a relative equality among the people. During those periods, interestingly enough, the Hebrew prophets were quite silent; they had little to say. But the archaeologists' diggings also uncover remnants of huge houses and little tiny hovels at other periods in the life of Israel, and other objects that show great economic disparities among the people. Not surprisingly, it's during those times when the prophets were most outspoken, denouncing the great gaps in wealth and the neglect of the poor. The Bible doesn't mind prosperity; it just insists that it be shared. Where are the prophets today?

Is Disney chief executive officer Michael Eisner really worth $97,000 per hour, when his workers in Haiti make about 28 cents an hour? Should market calculations be sufficient to value anyone that much more than others? People seem shocked to hear media reports that Michael Jordan made more from Nike in one year than all the workers in all the Asian factories that make Nike shoes did. But will shock lead to public discussion about the morality of such global disparities? The lack of capacity for social shame in our modern society is a worrisome problem. Somebody should be embarrassed by how quickly and easily the upper slice of Americans are now making money, while millions of American children endure third world living conditions. These growing economic gaps have a spiritual aspect: Americans are growing further and further apart. Therefore, the economic movement of the country works directly against all our spiritual traditions that would seek to bring us closer together.

The affluent, successful and attractive people who dominate television sitcoms and commercials are clearly not representative of society as a whole. Who is the target of an ad I saw recently in which a woman decides to buy a new refrigerator because she doesn't like the colour of the old one any more? It's a media illusion that almost everyone is enjoying the soaring market. For all the hype and hoopla about the economy, buying power seems to be more and more problematic for the majority. It seems to take more and more work from more and more people just to keep up.

In a society characterized both by extremes *and* a willingness to exclude significant numbers of people, all of us are in jeopardy. The old slogan 'There but for the grace of God go I' is truer than ever in the rapidly changing global economy. Even chief executive officers are no longer safe from corporate downsizing, to say nothing of the many top-level executives who have seen their personal fortunes change almost overnight when a new merger occurs. The threat of downsizing is ever present now, whereas it was not in my middle-class parents' experience. Average workers are in a more insecure position than they have been at any time since before unionization, and wages have been fairly stagnant for a long time. Many Americans are just a paycheque or two away from poverty, stuck in the precarious bottom of the middle class. And most of us could easily fall on hard times, with the loss of our job, health or family stability.

Thus, while poor people are still bearing the heaviest burden, working-class and even middle-class people are also living increasingly insecure lives. Most families need two incomes to support a middle-class life, or even a lower standard. Education for our children is often bad or incredibly costly. The quality and dependability of health care is eroding, even for people lucky enough to have insurance. While the top end of our society is reaping incredible bonanzas, the majority feel as if they're not making much progress, while those at the bottom are completely off society's radar screen except when they commit crimes. The neat categories of rich and poor don't adequately describe our economy any more; a new reality of middle- and working-class deprivation has entered the picture. Therefore, a society's commitment not to just leave people 'outside the gate' is an important commitment for everyone. The Harvard economist Richard Parker suggests we replace 'anti-poverty' work with broad and fair social policies that would improve the lives of not just the poor but the middle class as well.

Spiritual Poverty

Many Americans are searching for meaning and connection in our materialistic society. This is a sign of our second great poverty, which is *spiritual*. I have learned that it's a mistake to be so focused on the material poverty of the people at the bottom that we neglect or underestimate the spiritual impoverishment of those in the middle and even at the top. The booming economy is putting enormous pressure on all of us. Most families today must have two parents working full-time. There is less and less time for family, especially for the children, and for involvement in the community and institutions like the church and other voluntary associations.

The market also fuels a never-ending and relentless cycle of consumption, which not only undermines our personal integrity but destroys our sense of *moral* balance. We spend far too much time and energy thinking and worrying about 'things' and engaging in the constant activity of consumption. Whereas Descartes asserted, 'I think, therefore I am', modern advertising wants us to believe 'I shop, therefore I am'. When the shopping mall becomes the centre of life, the societal result is a deep crisis of meaning. The obvious insight no one wants to say out loud is that shopping simply doesn't satisfy the deepest longings of the human heart. And if work's only real purpose is to allow for more shopping, we have a formula for meaninglessness and, ultimately, despair.

Jesus's first temptation, while fasting in the desert, was to turn stones into bread. Here was the temptation of the easy answer, the quick fix, the instant solution. Why deny yourself...anything? Television commercials have much the same message today. You

can have all you ever wanted, and you can have it now! That was
the tempter's promise, and it is the lure of today's consumer culture.
But to more and more people in the modern corporate world, both
work and consumption feel increasingly meaningless – but there's
no time for anything but work and consumption. And that has
consequences: anxiety, stress, alienation and emptiness are some of
the most common.

Probably nothing I preach on the road has as much impact
as my recitation of Gandhi's 'seven deadly sins'. One Australian
radio talk-show host almost jumped out of his seat when he
first heard them. 'That's us!' he exclaimed. 'That's Australia;
that's the Western way of life.'

Gandhi used these warnings as a teaching tool, a primary
instruction for students at his ashram in India. The seven deadly
sins are these:

1 Politics without principle
2 Wealth without work
3 Commerce without morality
4 Pleasure without conscience
5 Education without character
6 Science without humanity
7 Worship without sacrifice

Gandhi's warnings go right to the heart of the values of the
culture we live in. They have become our way of life. Gandhi's
seven deadly sins are another way of describing our spiritual
poverty.

The economy may be booming, but how happy is life in the
gated communities? The poor aren't the only ones worried about
their kids; the affluent are worried about their children's values
or, worse, the consequences of their own values showing up in
their kids. It is no longer just the children of inner-city poverty
who are erupting in societal violence. Many of the shooting
sprees in junior high and high schools that have shocked
America were carried out by middle-class white kids from two-
parent homes. Listening to them talk, you quickly discover that
something has gone terribly wrong in their value system.
Selfishness and violence go together, especially in a society
whose popular culture regularly portrays violence as an easy
solution to our problems. When delayed gratification, hard work

or long-term preparation are antiquated values, and when the popular culture glorifies the ethic of taking what you want by any means necessary, the consequences will show up first in the young.

Our kids get the idea quickly. Late one night, I watched a winsome six-year-old being interviewed about his role in a Nike commercial alongside Michael Jordan. *Tonight Show* host Jay Leno asked the bright-eyed little boy if he wanted to be an athlete 'like Mike'. 'Oh, no,' replied the child star. 'I want to be an owner. I want the money without the sweat.' He's already learning the cultural message.

Jesus responds to the economic temptation in the desert by asserting, 'One does not live by bread alone.' Bread is not bad; on the contrary, bread is good and we need it. But there are much more important things, and all of our spiritual traditions say that. All human beings need security, but too much can be as dangerous as too little. Jesus later advises his followers to resist the temptations of the easy life, to be more modest and patient, to simplify their lives rather than to complicate them further, and to replace anxious striving with prayerful trust.

What's Most Important?

At a retreat for pastors I was leading one weekend, our spiritual poverty became readily apparent. A young Presbyterian pastor began to bare his soul, confessing that his training had not prepared him for what he was encountering in his parish. Most of his parishioners were corporate executives, lawyers or investment brokers who commuted every day from their suburban neighbourhoods to high-powered jobs in New York or Philadelphia. The youthful cleric wasn't judgemental toward them but was deeply concerned, telling us, 'They rise very early in the morning and are never back until late at night. Their credit cards are maxed out, they have no savings, and they must work constantly to maintain the lifestyles in which they're trapped. There is no time for family, community, church, or anything besides work and consumer activities. Marriages are on the rocks, kids are being neglected, alcoholism and other addictions are common, and spiritual life has long since died.' Then he was silent for a moment before he spoke again. 'I don't know how I can serve them!'

Across the room, a pastor on sabbatical from South Africa listened quietly. When no one else in the room responded to the young minister, the South African replied, 'You know, we too have many people who must get up very early in the morning and don't return home until late into the night. The buses come at 5 a.m. to bring them to the work sites and don't return them to their homes until 10 p.m. All they do is work, and there is little time left for family or anything else. Alcoholism and family breakdown are common. It causes great problems for the community and for the church. It seems like you have similar problems here in America. In South Africa, we call ours slave labour camps. It sounds like, in the United States, you have corporate labour camps.' The two pastors immediately understood each other.

What's most important? It's a question that troubles more and more people today. At a leadership training institute I attended, we were invited to go around the room and answer the question, What are you doing with your life? One participant responded, 'I sell salty snack foods.' This very successful manager and, I would discover, very nice person, seemed a little jolted by his own simple description of his life purpose. Answering that basic question of what we are doing with our lives can cause many a successful business, government or civic leader to take stock.

Of course, the middle class isn't the only one buffeted by the pressures of a consumer society. As if material poverty were not enough, poor people often suffer spiritual poverty as well. The same materialistic values so characteristic of America's affluent suburbs can be found just as readily in poor communities. Here, too, the influence of advertising and the popular culture take their toll. Indeed, one could argue that the negative influence of excessive consumerism can be even more destructive in places where people have so little to start with. On a recent trip to a shopping mall, I was pleased to find a pair of khakis on sale for $19.95. But when I asked the young sales clerk how to wash and dry them, he didn't know – he always had his dry-cleaned! It doesn't take much arithmetic to figure out how many times over this kid pays for his trousers – all just to maintain a certain crease and image somebody has convinced him is important.

John DiIulio, the social-policy analyst whom I spoke of earlier, describes a deep spiritual poverty among the most marginalized inner-city children. He describes it graphically as a kind of moral poverty. He points specifically to the large number of poor children who have almost no caring adults in their lives. Without any moral mentors or guiding influences, they are adrift in the middle of an ocean with no compass, surrounded by dangerous storms. 'In sum, moral poverty is the poverty of being without loving, capable, responsible adults who teach the young right from wrong. It is the poverty of being without parents, guardians, relatives, friends, teachers, coaches, clergy, and others who habituate (to use a good Aristotelian word) children to feel joy at others' joy, pain at others' pain, satisfaction when you do right, remorse when you do wrong.' DiIulio writes, 'It is the poverty of growing up in the virtual absence of people who teach these lessons by their own everyday example, and who lovingly insist that you follow suit and behave accordingly. In the extreme, it is the poverty of growing up severely abused and neglected, of being surrounded and hounded by deviant, delinquent, and criminal adults and other older youth in a social setting defined by dysfunctional homes, disorderly schools, and dangerous streets. To grow up in abject moral poverty is to grow up believing that impulsive violence or reckless behaviour is at least as right and rational as deferred gratification. It is to grow up feeling that cold-blooded exploitation is more natural than empathetic expression.'

Yes, there are other factors that turn well-loved teenagers into stone-cold killers. But, as DiIulio points out, 'It is more typically a lack of decent parents and other responsible adults that puts otherwise normal children behaviourally at risk, giving them little chance of becoming a civil, sober, skilled, and self-sufficient adult, and a better than average chance of engaging in crime, succumbing to the blandishments of alcohol and illegal drugs, remaining unemployed, and bringing into this world more children whose main patrimony is moral poverty.' The moral poverty DiIulio describes is a condition of the spiritual poverty we have been examining. It can also occur when there is no economic disadvantage present, and does so increasingly often as parenting and family life break down across the economic spectrum.

The latchkey syndrome of many affluent homes can produce similar moral poverty. The difference is this: the kids in the affluent suburbs of Virginia and Maryland, a few miles from where I live, have more to buffer the bad decisions that arise from their own spiritual poverty. They or their parents have many more resources to allow them second, third or endless chances to redeem themselves and turn their lives in a better direction after some initial bad choices. In effect, affluence often helps to mask moral and spiritual poverty. In my neighbourhood, in inner-city Washington, the bad choices kids make can quickly become matters of life and death. Sometimes there are no second chances for kids who are poor and whose families have no resources to buffer them. The spiritual poverty of poor people is often easier to see and harder to hide than that of the more affluent.

But there is yet another kind of poverty that increasingly affects us all.

Civic Poverty

The third great poverty is *civic* poverty – a decline in citizen participation in the political process, including voting, and an impoverishment of the political debate itself. During a lunch conversation on Capitol Hill, a member of Congress made a sad admission to the dozen of us seated around the table. 'We really haven't done anything this session,' he said. 'Only ten seats going the other way could change the party in control, and about 40 seats are at play in the autumn elections. That's really the only thing anyone is talking about up here. There's nothing else going on.'

I was asked to say a few words to wrap up the event and could respond only by reminding the group that a lot of other important things were going on in the rest of the country (the millions of families, for example, trying to make the difficult transition from welfare to work), and it was too bad that we weren't getting any help from Congress.

I know some dedicated elected officials who really would like to make a difference. But the system in which they operate has become so locked into rigidly polarized political debate that real answers to real problems can hardly be found. That fits the mood in most legislative bodies today, where politicians are looking not for solutions but just for people to blame. Winning elections and holding on to political power have clearly become ends unto themselves, with many lawmakers losing track of the reasons they are there. And winning requires an almost daily attention to fund-raising in order to meet the enormous costs of today's election campaigns. Money so controls the political process that it is no longer hyperbole to say that the votes of Congress are for sale.

The great casualty has been the very soul of democracy, and one vital danger sign is the appalling low and dropping levels of voting and political participation in the United States. Only half of us bother to vote in presidential elections today, compared with 80 per cent a century ago.

A Debate of Extremes

Along with the widespread public perception that special interest groups now dominate politics, there is a growing public disgust at the nature of the debate itself, and the role of the media in particular. Extreme views virtually control the political debate, and more and more of the nation is just tired of listening. The talking heads of the TV news shows seem to have opinions on every subject every day and seem to think that just being on television gives them some credibility or moral authority. They must hope that no one ever asks the obvious question: 'Just who are you people anyway, and what have you ever done that would make us want to hear what you have to say about this?'

Politics, like everything else, has become mere entertainment, and for that we need the clash of opposing opinions. But maybe some issues don't have just two opposing sides; maybe a variety of different angles and perspectives could help us find positive solutions. Instead, we see complex issues distorted in media-staged confrontations that virtually prevent the finding of any common ground.

I remember a request from one of the major networks to take part in such a staged battle. The National Religious Broadcasters Convention was in Washington, DC, and most of the major figures from the religious Right were in attendance. The network producer came to me with an idea. 'I've heard there's somewhere in the Bible where Jesus gets mad at religious leaders and tips tables over in a church. Is that true?' Well, sort of, I replied. I filled in a few of the details for him – how Jesus once confronted the leaders of the Jewish temple for commercializing and corrupting the house of worship. 'Great,' he said. 'That's what we have in mind. We'd like to film you walking into the convention centre looking very angry. You probably shouldn't knock over any of their tables, but you could storm up to [he named one of the religious Right's celebrities] and start an argument with him. We've already worked it all out with him, and he thinks it's a great idea!'

That's really what he said. Instead, I suggested that they bring the conservative Christian leader over to my apartment in the inner city (only blocks away from the luxurious convention centre) and film a conversation between us about the nature of Christian responsibility, especially to poor people. To their credit, that's exactly what they did, and the dialogue turned out to be quite constructive. The incident showed me again how addicted the media are to the two-sided confrontation, but also how a better dialogue can take place when that style of political discourse is challenged.

Listening to the rhetoric on both sides, you would think America is being forced to choose between the strategies of promoting family values or creating good jobs, between protecting the sacredness of life or defending the rights of women, between expanding economic opportunity or securing economic justice, between holding Hollywood accountable for its moral values or pressing large corporations to be responsible to their workers and communities, between upholding personal responsibility or working for racial equality. You would think, hearing the relentless conservative–liberal debate, that nobody could stand for all of the above, even though many Americans probably do.

Back to Marquis, my new nephew, adopted from the streets by my sister. He's a bit of a philosopher, so I asked him one day what he thought was meant by the now-famous African proverb 'It takes a village to raise a child', which he was writing a report on for school. I could tell he was thinking about this one carefully because he took a few moments to respond. 'Well,' he said, 'I guess it means that if I was outside playing and got all dirty and messed up and stuff, I could go to anyone's house to get cleaned up.' Not bad, I thought. Not bad at all.

Some months later, Marquis was watching one of the national political conventions on television. A presidential candidate had made a statement about child-rearing, and everybody was now arguing about it. The candidate exclaimed, 'It doesn't take a village; it takes a family!' The great liberal–conservative debate quickly ensued: Village! Family! Village! Family! Marquis just shook his head as he left the room and said to his parents, 'They just don't get the concept, do they?' No they don't, and because they don't, the public arena is dominated by a series of false choices that are killing our public discourse. This is civic poverty.

Just as was done during the era of the civil rights movement, a new generation could begin to apply our best moral or religious values to overcome the material and spiritual poverty that today shames and imprisons the soul of the wealthy countries. Together, we could also counter our civic poverty by searching for some real answers, instead of just finding more ways to argue over the questions. But that will require some soul-searching because the real issues are spiritual, not just political. And that realization is the beginning of both wisdom and transformation. In all that we do, we need to remember Chapter 5: Recognize the three faces of poverty.

Chapter Six

Listen to Those Closest to the Problem

'What do you want me to do for you?' Jesus asked him. The blind man said, 'Rabbi, I want to see.' (Mark 10.51)

MY WIFE TELLS THE STORY of a young priest facing a tough assignment – his first attempt to teach a Sunday school class. Eager to be accepted by the kids, he tried to portray himself as very casual and accessible. He sat on the edge of a desk and asked a question of the wide-eyed children. 'Hey kids,' he said, 'what's grey, furry, gathers nuts, and runs up and down trees?' There was a long pause while the kids looked at each other with puzzled faces. Finally, one little boy ventured an answer. 'Well, I know the answer should be Jesus... but it sure sounds like a squirrel to me!'

The story reminds us that there is not always an easy religious answer to every problem. Nevertheless, some of the most successful efforts in dealing with poverty and violence are emerging from faith communities – meaning not only churches and congregations, but a myriad of religiously and spiritually based nonprofit organizations. And many of those efforts teach us a clear lesson: Listen to those closest to the problem.

Boston is the site of the much-publicized Ten Point Coalition, sparked by the Revd Eugene Rivers. When Eugene Rivers's picture and the Boston story were featured on the cover of *Newsweek* in the summer of 1998, the nation got a glimpse of new possibilities for faith-based solutions to the problems of urban poverty, youth violence and crime. Eugene Rivers never expected such coverage by a national news magazine, and I remember the 2 a.m. phone call he made to tell me about it. But most stories don't begin on the cover of *Newsweek*, and this one didn't either.

Several years earlier, *Sojourners* began to report on *our* front cover what Gene and other black pastors were doing in Boston. Gene and I have carried on a 25-year-long conversation as his pilgrimage has taken him from street hustling in Philadelphia, to idea hustling in the academic halls of Harvard, and finally to Boston's tough Dorchester neighbourhoods, hustling to put his Pentecostal faith into practice. There, a heroin dealer gave some valuable advice to a handful of young black pastors who wanted desperately to do something to stop the violence on their streets and were willing to listen to anybody who might give them some ideas. The drug dealer said, 'When the kids get out of school, we're there and you're not. When they're out on the streets, we're there and you're not. When Mum sends Johnny out for a loaf of bread, we're there and you're not. All night long, we're there and you're not – so we win and you lose. It's as simple as that.' The pastors knew that the bars and crack houses were open to kids at virtually any hour of the day, while their churches were closed and locked most of the time.

Some months later, a now-famous incident in a Boston church served as the catalyst for change. On the night of 18 May 1992, a wake was being conducted at Morning Star Baptist Church for a young man named Robert Odom, who had been hit in the head by an errant bullet during a drive-by shooting. All of a sudden, some gang members burst into the sanctuary, pursuing a rival gang member who was at the wake. They started shooting and chased him around the church, finally stabbing him, right up near the pulpit. It's hard to get more dramatic than that. Several meetings of clergy and community leaders followed.

At one such meeting, the Revd Jeff Brown of Union Baptist Church warned, 'If the churches won't go into the streets, the streets will come into the churches.' At a later meeting, Eugene Rivers issued a clarion call, saying it was time for the clergy to go out and walk the streets, dealing with troubled young people on a one-to-one basis. Several established clergy laughed at the suggestion, and one jokingly suggested that Mr Rivers be appointed to lead the 'street committee'. 'All right,' said Gene, 'I will.' He then invited any pastor who was willing to join him to meet at his house the following Friday night, and they would start walking the streets together. Twelve showed up, and thereafter a small group of young pastors, in response to Rivers's invitation, started walking the streets at night, watching, listening, talking and establishing a crucial relationship with street youth. That was the beginning of what would become the Ten Point Coalition and, eventually, a *Newsweek* cover story. The drug dealer's insight and the stabbing in the church led to the formation of one of the most effective church-based efforts in the country at combating youth violence and offering concrete hope to shattered neighbourhoods in our urban communities.

Ten Point's approach is straightforward and simple – nothing will substitute for physical presence and unconditional but tough love. The churches make a very practical commitment to adopt gangs, local parks, particular blocks and street corners, and, most important, individual kids. The kids on the street have a sixth sense for consistency or lack thereof and are willing and eager to form natural kinships with anyone who seems to walk the walk and talk the talk. Committing to them is nothing less than a redemption strategy, block by block and kid by kid. In Boston and around the country, churches are beginning to divide up territory, just the way gangs do, to apply the love of God to the toughest neighbourhoods in America. And the results are impressive.

I was involved with the Ten Point Coalition from its inception and can testify to its very practical and close-to-home approach. It's really an old approach, but one that has escaped us in our age of professionalism and bureaucracy, even in the churches. It used to be that all the adults in a community felt a responsibility for bringing up the kids in the neighbourhood. You were as likely to be disciplined or looked after by somebody else's mum or dad as by your own. But as more and more families don't have both a mum and dad – especially a dad – and with role models disappearing in the communities where they are most needed, a lot of kids are just getting lost. Massive social welfare cutbacks, which have further abandoned many families to deeper poverty, have proved especially hard on at-risk youth. Add up all those factors and you have a recipe for disaster. Rivers cites studies claiming that by the year 2006, a large number of urban youth will reach the age at which criminal behaviour normally occurs. His commitment is for the churches to reach them before all the negative social forces do.

The Ten Point Coalition has formed new partnerships and made new allies, first between churches and then with other agencies, both public and private. Of critical importance was a new cooperation between inner-city pastors and the criminal justice system, with the police in particular. In the past, the Boston police had antagonized the black community by making wide sweeps that seemed to indiscriminately target young black men. Now the police backed off and, in cooperation with black ministers trusted in the community, focused on a much smaller group of hard-core perpetrators. The ministers offered repeat offenders a real chance to turn their lives around, but if their violent criminal behaviour continued, the ministers would assist the police in their arrest and incarceration. Jeff Brown, now one of the key urban leaders in Boston, says, 'Our commitment is always to work with these kids, but sometimes you have to work with them in a prison ministry for a while. We had to come to the realization that some of these young people are so out of control that the only way they will listen to you is if they're behind bars for a period of time.'

Obviously to play such a sensitive and difficult role, you have to know a community well – both the young people vulnerable to getting caught up in crime and their neighbours, who are the most frequent victims. You have to listen to those closest to the problem. And people have to trust you.

In Boston, where the police as well as the criminals are held accountable for their actions, the complaints against indiscriminate police harassment and abuse have gone way down. Boston has proved that such real community–police cooperation can work. In Boston today, the judges, police and politicians sing the praises of the black pastors who lead Ten Point, and credit collaboration with them for the city's significant reductions in youth crime and violence. The Revd Ray Hammond, the chair of Boston's Ten Point Coalition, says, 'We have demonstrated success in preventing the violence that was devastating our communities. But now our focus is on the development of real alternatives to violence and crime in the lives of these young people.' Ray and his wife, Gloria White Hammond, are pastors of the Bethel African Methodist Episcopal (AME) Church, where they are pioneering many very successful programmes, such as mentoring for young teenage girls to prevent unwanted pregnancies. And the Ella Baker House, the impressive ministry of Eugene Rivers's Azuza Christian Community in Dorchester's Four Corners neighbourhood, has become a model for youth ministry around the country. Gene has now created the National Ten Point Leadership Foundation, a network of black church-based ministries in a dozen cities.

Jeff Brown was one of the original young pastors who first started walking the streets of Boston. He talks about the partnerships that have been forged. 'The Boston success story is not a solo act. It is a choir, where police officers talk about jobs and economic parity, clergy talk about law enforcement, social workers talk about the importance of spiritual uplift, and the private sector talks about street-level intervention. It is a choir that harmonizes on the melody of community resurrection.'

Essential to the success that the Boston pastors have found is listening to the right people, in particular to the kids on the street. Eugene Rivers's disdain for listening to the experts, the politicians, and even the leaders of the big-steeple churches, rather than the kids, has often landed him in trouble. But while his strident criticism of others has sometimes been controversial, his commitment to listening to the kids on the street is right on target.

The Ten Point Coalition's success stems in part from its unapologetic spiritual basis. The poor urban youth are not just clients: they are the children of God, deserving of God's redemptive love. Street kids are not just participating in a programme but rather are entering into relationships that are offering to help them change their lives. The pastors and youth workers who become involved are not in this for the money or their careers; they do it because they believe God has called them. Both the motivation of the workers and the possibility of spiritual transformation offer a much greater potential for success than more secular and bureaucratic social programmes can normally provide. A spiritually based effort is more likely to listen to poor people themselves.

Whom Do You Trust?

Whom do we listen to and whom do we trust? *Trust* is essential to listening. Why do we continue to believe the myth that poor people don't know anything and can't be trusted? Where do you really find more truth about a society – at the top or at the bottom? Are the best solutions conceived in the corridors of power or in the neighbourhoods? Do the poor really have no assets or resources, as most people think? Listening to the poor opens up whole new possibilities, ideas and directions in overcoming poverty.

Why listen to the poor? Well, there are good biblical and ethical reasons. But there are also just plain practical reasons. Many youth-

and community-serving programmes have found what Ten Point discovered: they couldn't get off the ground until they began to truly trust and engage and involve the people they were trying to serve. Many good and decent programmes didn't become highly successful until the poor themselves were given a real hearing and became involved in their leadership. The presence of the poor in the discussion makes all the difference. I can testify to this fact. When young people are at the table for a discussion of youth violence and what to do about it, the conversation is very different from what it would be otherwise. Too often, the discussions we have about poverty involve only the people who are working to overcome it.

The Revd Sam Mann, a pastor and key figure in the Kansas City gang peace summit, wants to 'raise the bar of inclusivity'. He says those from the dominant social groups are going to have to learn to give up some of their control and their icons if we are really to have a new table around which everyone can meet. John DiIulio once told me his three principles for solving the country's worst societal problems: 'One: Trust those closest to the problem. Two: Trust those closest to the problem. Three: Trust those closest to the problem.'

Nearly every time I talk to Nane Alejandrez, he tells me he has 'revised the business plan' and that he also has taken some more young people from the barrio up into the mountains for a sweat (a Native American prayer ceremony conducted around burning coals in a makeshift tent called a sweat lodge). Daniel 'Nane' Alejandrez was once a drug addict, felon and veteran of barrio warfare in California. He had seen scores of family members either die on the streets or end up in prison. But Nane had a spiritual conversion. He is now the director of Barrios Unidos, perhaps the most effective anti-violence youth organization working in Latino communities across the nation.

Barrios is involved in a myriad of youth activities and projects for community-based economic development. It is creating T-shirt and silk-screening businesses, computer centres, job-training projects, art shows, and alternative schooling. And it's working to steer street kids away from gangs and into positive community service. The young Barrios warriors are committed to a powerful combination of economic and spiritual development.

But because Nane was from the streets (and had the tattoos to prove it), no bank or credit union would give Barrios the initial investment capital it needed. Nane invited me to Santa Cruz, California, to see their activities and hear their exciting plans to expand. I was very impressed. 'How much do you need to get this up and running?' I asked him. Nane wanted only $30,000 of loan capital but had no connections to get even that small amount. So I arranged a meeting with Gaylord Thomas, a savvy streetwise organizer himself, on the national staff of the Evangelical Lutheran Church in America. The Lutheran Church made a very important decision: they listened to Nane, took a chance on a grassroots leader and programme, and made Barrios a business loan with accompanying technical assistance. Barrios Unidos is now in more than 24 states across the country and is developing a whole new generation of Latino leadership. The city of Santa Cruz has helped Barrios to obtain almost a whole block in which to expand its successful operations. The Lutherans trusted the people closest to the problem, and never did they make a better investment.

In addressing problems like youth violence, addiction, family breakdown and teenage pregnancy, face-to-face relationships engaging those closest to the problem have clearly worked far better than bureaucratic approaches. Even in the tough areas of housing, job creation and environmental clean-up, smaller-scale and community-based programmes are demonstrating results. And new community-policing efforts, in partnership with community-based groups, are helping to turn many neighbourhoods around. But these close-to-home solutions work far better when they have the support of larger institutions in the wider community. Investing our time, energy, and money in such hopeful initiatives, started by those closest to the problem, is one of the best roads to social change.

Poor People, Not the Poor

Mary Nelson hates it when people refer to 'the poor'. She would rather speak of the new relationships through which all of us can participate in the exciting task of community development. In the West Side Chicago neighbourhood of Garfield Park, the efforts of her Bethel New Life community organization powerfully demonstrate what low-income people can do if they mobilize their own resources. Mary Nelson is neither a black inner-city pastor nor a Latino community organizer but a white-haired Lutheran church lady with a powerful vision.

But that vision came out of listening to and forming relationships with the residents of an impoverished and forgotten local community. When Mary arrived in 1965 to support her brother David Nelson as the new pastor of Bethel Lutheran Church, things were very different.

'Three days after we got here, there were riots,' she says. Two years later, the neighbourhood had gone from 95 per cent white to 90 per cent black through the red-lining policies of banks and the block-busting tactics of real-estate agents who use race and fear to quickly change neighbourhoods. When the turbulence subsided, the church had dwindled to 35 elderly members, the remnant of the ethnic German population who had fled Garfield Park with the arrival of African Americans. But the Nelsons stayed. Pastor Nelson knew that the only way to break into the rapidly changed parish was to literally go door-to-door and ask new residents, 'How can we help?' The neighbours whom the Nelsons won over and the black youth who came to sing in the choir transformed Bethel into the church of 600 members that it is today. 'They call us a Lutheran-Baptist church,' says Mary, smiling.

A housing crisis in the community gave Bethel its first mission. Mary recalls, 'We looked around and said, "Man, we'd better do something about housing or there won't be a neighbourhood left to be a church in." So with no money and no plan of action, we felt called by God to try and do housing.' And they did. So far 900 units of housing have been constructed or rehabilitated through Bethel's efforts.

But what began as an effort to rebuild the community's housing stock soon became much more, as the need for long-term neighbourhood sustainability became clear. Bethel New Life, with Mary Nelson at the helm, transformed itself into an engine of comprehensive community development, creating new initiatives in education, employment, health care, senior and child care, transitional living for people who were homeless, and even an 'incubation programme' to assist budding entrepreneurs in getting new local businesses off the ground. Bethel has become one of the area's largest job providers, creating meaningful work for hundreds of people. A closed local hospital is currently being transformed into a new community centre offering everything from preschool to the performing arts.

Mary draws lessons from the Bible about community organizing. At one of our Call to Renewal national roundtables, she led the morning devotions around a New Testament passage, Mark 2.1–12. Some men bring a sick friend to a house where Jesus is, so he can be healed. But the crowds are too large, and they cannot get near Jesus. So they cut a hole in the roof of the house and lower their sick friend, on his pallet, down into the room where Jesus is. Jesus speaks to him, and he is healed. She spoke of the need for teamwork and explained that every project requires an initiator (the visionary who came up with the idea of cutting a hole in the roof), implementers (those who made it happen by carrying the stretcher up to the roof and cutting the hole), intercessors (those who lead the way in prayer), and investors (those who supply the capital – someone had to buy the stretcher!).

Like Eugene Rivers and Nane Alejandrez, Mary Nelson organizes with a vibrant spirituality. She says that the 'four G's' help keep Bethel New Life going. It's the 'glue' of Christian community that keeps them all together, against anything that would tear them apart. It's the 'gasoline' from the Sunday liturgy refuelling stop, where community members are reminded that 'despite setbacks, God is going to bring us through'. It's the 'guts' that helps in making tough but effective decisions (like mortgaging the church buildings to begin the first housing programme). And it's the 'grace' to remind them that while it takes hard skills to accomplish things, 'it is faith that drives us'. Like most good organizers, Mary Nelson has a well-developed theology of hope – you've got to when you face the threat of hopelessness every day. 'You're always hovering between "Boy, we're going to get this done", and "Boy, this is a terrible problem and there's nothing we can do about it"', she says, 'and a vociferous voice will lead you either way.' But then the church lady turned streetwise organizer explains her bedrock faith: 'The only way you can respond to that kind of thing is to say that the eyes of faith won't label anything as hopeless. God will make a way; God will help us find a way, and then you celebrate the victories and you mourn the losses and you move forward.' Having worked with her on many a project, I can tell you that Mary Nelson is always moving forward, working side by side with the people of her neighbourhood.

Poor people have resources, Mary insists, contrary to what most people think. Bethel's asset-based approach to organizing in a poor neighbourhood has produced real results. The resources that poor communities have – time, energy, numbers,

relationships, experience, talent, faith and even some money –
when pooled together, can become very significant. Bethel has
successfully forged economic development in the kind of place
where most people give up. Mary will tell you that we still have
many misconceptions about the causes and consequences of
material poverty. The idea that poor people have no assets is a
myth; the problem is how to mobilize those assets. A whole
network based around the concept of asset-based community
development is taking hold around the country. The concept
asserts that poor people and communities are rich sources of
assets and gifts that must be recognized, developed, and
mobilized. The goal is sufficiency, self-determination and
productivity for those who are now poor.

But listening to those closest to the problem means that you have
to be close enough to hear. And doing that can sometimes be a little
scary. Mary tells the story of a very bad period of horrific violence in
their West Side Chicago community. Gangs, drugs, guns and vicious
territorial battles were taking a deadly and mounting toll. Unsure of
exactly what to do, several women from Bethel New Life decided to
conduct a simple prayer vigil right on a corner where several young
people had been shot. They chose to do it all night, right through
the most dangerous hours. A small circle of women began their vigil
one hot summer evening, carrying white crosses with the names of
those who had died written on them. Fewer than a dozen women
continued to stand alone on the street corner as the hour got later
and later. Around midnight, with nobody else around, they spotted
a group of young gang members heading their way. Swallowing
hard, the Bethel women continued their prayer and singing. One of
the young men walked right up to them and challenged, 'Where's
Cinque?' More than a little frightened, the women asked who Cinque
was. He was a good friend who had been shot, the young man
replied. 'You forgot Cinque,' he said. 'Well, let's make a cross for
Cinque, then,' said Mary, and added, 'perhaps you would like to join
our vigil for a while.' Amazingly enough, they did join the vigil that
night, holding the cross with their friend's name on it. Standing there
together in the middle of the night on that deserted street corner, the
young men and the women began to talk. It was the beginning of a
relationship that would see some of those young people become
personally involved in the work of the Bethel community. But only
those willing to stand close enough to listen will ever hear those
closest to the problem.

Listening to those closest to the problem doesn't mean you don't use every resource from wherever you can get it to solve those problems. Mary and her co-workers have also learned how to work the system for some of the resources they need to complement their own community efforts. Both government and business recognize success when they see it, as evidenced by the $2.7 million welfare-to-work grant the US Labor Department gave Bethel New Life to develop even more jobs. The results come when we realize that poor people should be defined not merely by what they need but by what they can do.

Overcoming poverty, not simply servicing it, is the vision to strive for. To do anything less not only is patronizing but creates dynamics of dependency and control. Effective organizing has as its goal the prophetic biblical vision of Isaiah for people who have been oppressed: 'They shall build houses and inhabit them, they shall plant vineyards and eat their fruit. They shall not build and another inhabit, they shall not plant and another eat; for like the days of a tree shall my people be, and my chosen shall long enjoy the work of their hands. They shall not labour in vain, or bear children in calamity; for they shall be offspring blessed by the Lord.' The prophet Micah, too, offers a compelling image for those who have been left behind: 'They shall all sit down under their own vines and fig trees, and no one shall make them afraid.'

When We Don't Listen

But we usually don't listen to the poor. On the contrary, it's easy to pick on poor people, to simply blame the poor for their poverty. We do it all the time. But living and working with those who are poor gives you a whole different perspective.

Thelma used to live next door. She and her family were there before we arrived in the neighbourhood some 20 years ago. Thelma's husband had died, so the responsibility of keeping the family together fell to her. And she did it well. Three generations grew up in that house with, as far as we could see, good family values.

But because Thelma could never afford a down payment, she could never buy her house. One of our tenant organizers sat down with Thelma one day, and they figured out that she had paid for her place several times over in rent. Over the years, she was the most stable figure in the ever-changing history of a house that had had several owners during the period of her residence. The last owner was the DC government, which had done nothing to help Thelma own her own home. Instead, without fixing the plumbing or a leaking roof, they had raised the rent again. Thelma just couldn't afford it. One day, when I came home from a long trip, I was shocked to see that Thelma had moved out and her place had been boarded up. Ever since, we've had to fight to keep it from becoming a rat-infested crack house.

Thelma never got the equity from her housing investment that might have helped put her kids through college. She never received the home ownership mortgage tax deduction, a far bigger entitlement for the middle class than welfare is for the poor. And she never could get the parental help that many middle-class folk receive – a loan for the down payment on their first home. Listening to people like Thelma taught our community organizers more about the housing problem in America than attending meetings at the Department of Housing and Urban Development ever did.

There is a parable here. It's about class, race and the economic system. It's not about Thelma's failures. Sure, poor people can make bad choices that entrench them in poverty. But there's more to it than that. In fact, as I said earlier, bad personal choices can have far more severe results for the poor than for the well-off. That's why we are very tough at Sojourners Neighborhood Center about young people making the right choices in life and not further compounding the poverty they started with.

But there are always social and structural reasons why some people are poor and others are not. For example, it would not be difficult for America to figure out a fair way for low-income families to buy their own homes, and that would make a great difference in the fight to overcome poverty. But we have *chosen* not to do it.

The Bible sees those societal choices as moral failures. Instead of ignoring the poor, it tells us, we should listen to them, pay attention to them, and even evaluate our success as a society by how we treat them. It's not that poor people are different from or better than anyone else. Not at all. Living and working in some of the poorest neighbourhoods in this country for 25 years has taught me that those at the bottom have all the good and bad in them that people do anywhere else. But from a moral viewpoint, those at the bottom are the litmus test for the health of the whole society. That is both a religious insight and the beginning of

political wisdom. If you want to really know the truth about a
society, look to its bottom rungs. The perspective is clearer there
and less subject to varnish and illusion. That's where you find out
what is really going on and how best to change it. You are
unlikely to learn it in any other place because, in part, the political
and media centres that disseminate information about society
don't want people to really know what is happening at the
bottom. An honest view from the bottom is usually uncomfortable
for those at the top.

Our traditional approach to the problems of poverty has been
far too bureaucratic. We don't talk about the meaning of
community, we just engage in endless arguments over resources
and allocations. Now we've created a whole poverty industry, a
professional social welfare bureaucracy that is rich in procedures
and regulations but poor in genuine compassion and real
connection to people. Unless we discover a new sense of family
and community, we will never face our issues of poverty and
racism. Where will we find the reconciling practices to bring the
disparate parts of the family together? How do we begin saying
'we' instead of talking about 'us' and 'them'? Developing the big
'we' will take a common vision and strategy 'that will resonate
around our kitchen table', as the veteran anti-poverty organizer
Tom Jones puts it. He says, 'Our great national initiatives in civil
rights, women's rights and the environment drew upon our
collective social conscience, our sense of justice and fairness, and
our confidence in creating opportunities. But it's been different
with poverty.'

Jones says candidly, after four decades of grassroots organizing
and coalition building, 'I think we have, in the end, attempted to
resolve poverty with networks of professionals working in a well-
meaning yet palliative social welfare industry, allocating an
inadequate amount of resources to make life barely endurable for
the poor. We didn't end poverty, we serviced it. Notwithstanding
the billions of dollars and armies of workers and professionals (I
include myself and most of my life's work), we must admit that
after four decades, we are left with three significant facts: the
quality of life for today's poor is as bad as, if not worse than, it
has ever been; the separation and segregation of the poor from
the rest of this nation is greater than ever; and more Americans
than ever are either denying the degree and extent of poverty in
America, or simply don't care.' Jones calls for a commitment that

moves beyond the provision of social services 'to invigorate a sense of emotion, drama, and outrage around the issues of poverty and racism.'

Mobilizing a New Alliance

That commitment will require a mobilization that touches every part of the community. It is a natural role for the religious community to transcend its own social-service mentality and remember its prophetic calling to seek justice. But it must go beyond the churches to engage the arts, media, academia, business and political leadership, and the hundreds of thousands of community and civic organizations – the civil society – that shape much of our social life. The task is simple to generate a new expression of compassion and resolution on behalf of poor people that connects them to the rest of us. It's about including people in the family and the body politic.

What will it ultimately take to overcome poverty? It simply won't happen until we see 'the poor' as friends and neighbours, even brothers and sisters, who are not yet known to us. That will take relationship, partnership and risk more than care, subsidy and services. It will require our institutions to invest their assets, not just their surplus, and engage the gifts and talents of all their members, not just the leaders. It will require new ways of thinking and acting on the part of all of us. And it will take a reweaving of social relationships in our families and churches, as well as in our schools and workplaces. We must learn to perceive the poor not as a problem to be overcome but as precious resources that have been ignored – people who have gifts and talents that would extend and enrich the community once they were permitted to sit as friends and neighbours in the circles of our lives. Churches and other social institutions must learn to measure poverty by the numbers of children and families who are left outside their doors by a lack of welcome, as much as they are left outside the society by bad national policies. Ultimately, a social climate of shame should apply to those institutions and social bodies who will not come to terms with the 'least' of our people, as Jesus would say.

Many of the successful social movements that have made a difference in history result from an alliance between middle-class people and poor people. Without the insight that comes from viewing a society from the bottom up and without the energy of the oppressed, middle-class advocates can't really understand what needs to be changed, nor do they have a constituency that demands it. And without the resources and access that the middle class brings, poor people often don't have the voice to finally make a difference. The abolitionist and civil rights movements in the United States were good examples of alliances of the middle class and the poor, as are the myriad democratic movements in Latin America, Eastern Europe and South Africa. Nothing is more satisfying than being part of a movement like that, one that anyone who wants to can join.

We know that government cannot alone solve the problem of poverty. Real solutions will need involvement from all of us. It's difficult to get many different groups working together, but the principle of partnership is this – everybody does their share, and everyone does what they do best. Nobody gets to sit on the sidelines, and everyone brings some answers and some resources. It can work; I've seen it over and over again. Always, the key is listening to those closest to the problem.

Chapter Seven

Get to the Heart of the Matter

For our struggle is not against enemies of blood and flesh,
but against the rulers, against the authorities, against the cosmic
powers of this present darkness, against the spiritual forces of evil
in the heavenly places. (Ephesians 6.12)

THE WORD 'RADICAL' is widely misused and misunderstood. Its meaning goes back to 'radix', or 'root' (of the problem), but today it is merely a synonym for extremism. Too bad. Too many people are willing to address only the symptoms of problems and never get to the heart or root causes. We need to do more than pull people out of the river before they drown; someone needs to go upstream to see who or what is throwing them in. Asking why so many people are poor, why the affluent are so unhappy, or why the political process seems to be broken can get you into trouble, but also might lead to some real solutions.

I'll never forget a visit to our Sojourners Community from Archbishop Dom Helder Câmara of Brazil. The courageous cleric had become a champion for the poor in Latin America and throughout the world. Though in his mid-seventies, he wanted to walk the streets of our inner-city Washington, DC, neighbourhood and was full of questions about the life of its people. After listening intently to my description of housing patterns that were displacing poor people for the benefit of wealthy real estate speculators and affluent home buyers, Dom Helder shook his head knowingly. 'It's the same way in Recife', the poor city in northeastern Brazil where he resided. I recalled a statement he had made years before: 'When I feed the poor, they call me a saint. But when I ask why they are poor, they call me a communist.' Communism is no longer the issue it once was, but the archbishop's question still generates great controversy. Asking 'why' can lead you to the heart of the problem.

I also had the great blessing of meeting Dorothy Day several times. She was the founder of the Catholic Worker movement and became the conscience of the Catholic Church in her time. The Catholic Workers set up houses of hospitality, serving poor and homeless people across the country with works of mercy. More than 100 Catholic Worker houses are still flourishing today, feeding the hungry and sheltering the homeless. It's easy to get caught up in the immediate when you are doing intense work with poor people because it's so difficult just to keep things going. But Dorothy always made sure the *Catholic Worker* newspaper spoke out against systems that made people poor, attitudes that divided them by race, and governments that turned them into cannon fodder in times of war.

Through their publication, public protest and campaigns of nonviolent direct action, the Catholic Worker movement offered a prophetic witness alongside their works of mercy. In the opening scene from the movie about her life, *Entertaining Angels*, Dorothy is in jail for opposing H-bomb tests, and a poor and desperate woman is thrown into the cell with her. The picture of Dorothy Day cradling the frightened and crazed woman in her arms is a moving portrait of a moral leader who told the truth about political and economic power *and* took responsibility for the victims of that abusive power.

Dorothy was a mentor for me and taught me valuable lessons about the courage it takes to be prophetic, to speak to the deeper causes of things. She also showed me the importance of staying close to those who are victimized by power, instead of getting too cosy with the powers that be. Those in political power will often offer a kind of access to leaders of social movements, but it is often an access without content. The powerful may like to listen to your ideas and even read your books, but that may not lead to any meaningful changes. Talking to you makes them feel as if they're doing something, and they hope that might satisfy you, too. But it can't. I've learned that personal notes from politicians and presidents mean very little after your criticisms of their behaviour appear in the *New York Times*.

The biblical prophets were not hesitant to challenge the rulers of their day. That task generally found them in the desert (the usual location for the biblical prophets) rather than in the corridors of power, where the king's false court prophets resided – the advisers who just told him what he wanted to hear. It's always safer for your soul to be arrested for protest outside the White House than to be invited in for breakfast. Having experienced both, I find the former perhaps less comfortable but much less dangerous. A little quote from Dorothy Day hangs on the wall of my study: 'Most of our problems stem from our acceptance of this filthy, rotten system.' Perhaps not very poetic, but the sentiment is a crucial reminder to anyone seeking social change.

No matter what our personal involvement is in the small and practical efforts to make change close to home, it is vitally important that we join with wider movements and campaigns to protest and challenge the larger forces that wreak such havoc in the lives of so many people, especially the poor. Such movements are always made up of ordinary people like us, and our involvement in them provides the broader context and credibility that our local efforts need.

To get to the heart of the matter, an activist sometimes needs to learn a little theology. William Stringfellow, a lawyer and Episcopal lay theologian, was a great teacher to a whole generation of activists looking for a deeper analysis of social and political problems. He explained theologically what I had learned in Sociology 101: that an institution is more than the sum of its parts and that it carries an ethos and spirit of its own. Stringfellow brought back to American religious and political conversation the biblical notion of 'principalities and powers'. He reminded us of the biblical theology that posits that institutional structures – governmental, corporate and even religious – have a spiritual reality underneath their outward social and political manifestations. I recall many a conversation around Stringfellow's dining-room table when his theological analysis of political institutions shed great light on a political problem we were wrestling with.

The Market and the Common Good

'Big mergers, soaring corporate profits, record salaries for CEOs and starting pitchers, but thousands of job layoffs for American workers. Happy holidays – here's your pink slip!' So began a column I wrote as Christmas 1998 approached, and a record year

for the American economy also became a record year for job
layoffs. What's wrong with this picture, I asked, and why was
almost nobody putting the two together? Why does Wall Street
profit, while workers and their families must take a hit?

From computer giants to the world's biggest oil companies,
merger has become the favourite sport of the world's corporate
and financial elites. Those who run the economy agree on one
thing – bigger is better.

When Exxon purchased Mobil, creating the biggest and richest
company in the world, the historic antitrust victory of 1911 that
broke up the oil empire of John D. Rockefeller was reversed. But
Wall Street seems to be exempt from moral scrutiny. Costs must
be cut, said the new company's executives. What's the easiest way
to do that? Cut more jobs.

Throughout the 1990s, the wave of layoff announcements
made grim holiday seasons for tens of thousands of workers.
Company after company laid off long-serving and loyal workers,
all in the name of being more profitable and competitive.
Shareholder profits seemed to be the only bottom line for these
business corporations.

Let's take a look at some of the recurring facts of our economic
life today:

- Mergers are in, with new consolidations occurring every day.
- Costs are being slashed by the new supercompanies, with job
  layoffs as the favourite tactic.
- Almost every time jobs are cut, the companies' value goes up
  on Wall Street.
- And every time mergers happen and jobs are cut, the salaries
  of top executives go up.

Now consider the moral dimension of these economic realities. I
know nobody does this – it involves the stock market, which is not
supposed to be judged by any moral standards. The market is the
great given; it's just what is. But do we really want to live that way?
Few things impact our lives more than the economy. So why do
we continue to exempt economic behaviour from moral scrutiny?
Even the best business schools will now tell you that there are
other stakeholders involved in business decisions – workers,
customers, consumers, the community as a whole, the environment's well-being and even future generations. But most of those

other factors don't fare well with the increasing dominance of quarterly profit-and-loss statements.

Catholic social teaching has a useful concept known as the common good: individual benefits are not enough to evaluate a society or its practices; rather, we need to be looking after the needs of the whole community, especially those who most easily are left behind. That's the common good.

But who was looking after the common good in the Exxon–Mobil merger? Can anybody seriously suggest that bigger, more powerful and more profitable corporations will help to protect the interests of workers, consumers, the environment, local communities and the forgotten poor? Is it right that the casino economy of Wall Street profits when the real economy of workers and their families suffers? Is it fair that the people who do the firing get a rise, while the people fired can only fear for the future of their families? But 'right' and 'fair' are not words that the market economy wants to bring into this conversation.

For some time now, I've been carrying on a private dialogue with a major leader of the religious Right on many subjects, including economic justice. While we didn't agree on many things, he was remarkably sensitive to the issues of corporate downsizing and their effect on working-class families, even though he was the first to admit that his natural political allies in the corporate world didn't share that sensitivity. After several conversations, he shared with me that his working-class father had once lost his job, through no fault of his own. He remembered his dad crying at the kitchen table about it. It was still a personal issue for this conservative Christian leader, and it shaped his views of responsible and irresponsible corporate behaviour. Don't ever let markets and politics exempt themselves from moral scrutiny. Raise the realities of what their behaviour does to people's lives. Challenge the ethical foundations of their decision making. Get to the heart of the matter by raising the values questions.

Race and Repentance

We cannot answer the question of whether we are getting to the root of our problems without also looking again at the persistent issue of race in America. Today, a shallow concept of 'multiculturalism' may actually be hindering our progress. Just

enjoying one another's music and restaurants is hardly enough.
And the approach that 'people of all colours are racists and need
to repent' is neither good theology nor honest history. In the
deepest and most honest sense, the real issue at stake in American
racial history is the idolatry of white supremacy.

The persistence of white identity itself, with the accompanying
assumption of white privilege, is still the major obstacle to real
change in the racial climate. Italians, Swedes, Irish and Germans,
for example, were never a common ethnic group, but all became
'white people' when they arrived in America. What does that
mean? When I ask that question in audiences of white Americans,
a new recognition often occurs. I make a joke about how Germans
are pretty much like the Irish, and Italians can hardly be told apart
from Swedes. 'All the Europeans were pretty much the same,
weren't they?' I ask. After the laughter subsides, I ask, 'Why then,
when you came to America, did you all become "white people"?'
There is no white history or culture or country. Race is not rooted
in either biology or culture. It is a political construct, created for a
social purpose.

Indeed, the 'white race' was and is merely a political
construction to supply an ideology, first for slavery and then for
discrimination. That ideology must be dismantled if racial
progress is to be made in America. And because the ideology of
the white race is also an idolatry that challenges our true and
common identity as the children of God, its exorcism is a spiritual
and theological necessity.

More than 30 years after the death of Dr Martin Luther King, Jr,
America is still divided along racial lines. Why?

The facts: two-thirds of black Americans have achieved middle-
class status 30 years after the civil rights movement, but one-third
remain in poverty – many seemingly trapped in the social
pathologies of the urban underclass. At the same time, the
increase in the number and profile of other racial minorities is
dramatically changing the country's demographic landscape and
enormously complicating America's increasingly colourful racial
picture. And while many whites are still poor, poverty continues
to be disproportionately the experience of people of colour in
America, especially among the millions of their children who have
just been abandoned.

But racism is more than poverty. In 2002, middle-class African-
American, Latino, Asian and Native American parents are still able

to tell personal stories of racial prejudice and discrimination directed at them or their children. Most white people, on the other hand, seem tired of talking about racism, are opposed to affirmative action and want to believe that their country has now become a level playing field for all races. Few people of colour believe that. Most significantly, the United States is still a very segregated society – from residential patterns to cultural associations to church attendance. The number of stable, racially integrated neighbourhoods across the country is still pitifully small. And after school or work, people of different races in America spend precious little time together.

Have we made progress since the end of legal segregation? Undeniably. But have we come as far in the 30 years since the civil rights revolution as most of us expected we would? Obviously not. Most people today would probably agree that the hopes and dreams that followed the passage of the historic 1960s civil rights and voting rights legislation have yet to be fulfilled. As we enter a new century, America is still a racially divided society, where diversity is widely perceived as a cause for conflict more than for celebration. The question is why?

Clearly we underestimated the problem. Since the 1960s, we have learned that racism goes deeper than civil rights and, indeed, has survived the civil rights movement. Many social analysts and commentators have persuasively argued that racism goes deeper than mere prejudice and personal attitudes and is rooted in institutional patterns and structural injustices. At the end of his life, Dr King was himself more focused on the issues of poverty, which, he believed, were the next front in the battle to overcome racism.

The depth of racism in the cultural and psychological history of the United States has seldom been fully comprehended. Especially underestimated has been the impact and enduring legacy of the institution of slavery in America. Perhaps we have yet to get to the heart of the problem because we have failed to perceive the fundamental spiritual and theological roots of racism in America.

In biblical terms, racism is an idol that enslaves people and nations in its deadly grip. An idol is simply a lie that people believe and worship. It's the idol of 'whiteness' and the assumptions of white privilege and supremacy that have yet to be spiritually confronted in America, and even in the churches. White racism truly is America's 'original sin', to use an old theological concept bound up in the very founding of the nation. Building a nation on land stolen from indigenous people, with the use of slave labour from kidnapped black Africans, has left us with a legacy we have yet to fully deal with. The lack of true repentance for that sin still confounds our efforts to overcome it.

There is more to do than educating, organizing, advocating, changing consciousness and changing policies. A more spiritual approach would suggest other kinds of action as well. In addition to the hard work of personal relationships, community building and political and economic change, other responses may be required – like confession, prayer, conversion and forgiveness. White privilege is hard to give up, and racial oppression is hard to forgive.

Will we move beyond dialogues and presidential commissions and commit ourselves to the personal relationships, institutional transformations and social and political policies that would move us from soft multiculturalism to a racially pluralistic democracy? It's still difficult to get to the heart of any matter in America without probing the issues of race.

Homelessness and Compassion

While in Boston, I observed how the city's activists for the homeless are developing a comprehensive strategy, and seem to be getting a new kind of cooperation from many sectors of the community. First, the media have been engaged. I've never heard more radio shows designed to educate the public about the problem of homelessness. Engaging guests, such as a doctor who has devoted his life to serving the homeless or a street counsellor who goes out from the shelters to find people on the streets, offer compelling and informative testimonies about the problem. Patiently, these activists answer callers' questions about the nature of homelessness and the homeless in ways that generate both compassion and understanding. They provide powerful examples of offering direct help and service to the myriad personal problems that homeless people face.

At the same time, the activists are also strong advocates for public policy change, challenging local and state officials with reliable statistics about the problem (e.g. how many people have died on the streets of Boston this winter because of the cold) and recommending concrete policy alternatives. They have even gained the cooperation of the police, who are often very hostile and brutal to homeless people in many other cities. In Boston, the police are trying to become caring instead of cruel, to quote one homeless activist. The street counsellors and homeless shelters are now coordinating with the police to find and offer concrete help and services to people without a place to live.

On one local radio show, the audience was enlisted to help find and serve homeless people by calling the police whenever they saw someone who seemed to be living on the street. The callers were assured that the police would work with the street counsellors to assist and care for the people they found. 'You can help us find the people who need our community's help', listeners were told. I had never heard that before. They're working with the personal problems of homeless people, coordinating a public response and advocating to change public policy – all to transform the lives of homeless people and families. Here is a community trying to work together to solve the problem of homelessness. All this is the result of leadership that insists on getting to the heart of the matter.

To get to the heart of the matter, we must deal with both the personal and the political. That's the picture of Dorothy Day in the prison cell, consoling a poor woman whom the system had just thrown away while she was protesting against the system itself. An inspiring mentor, she never settled for easy answers but instead always asked hard questions. We should too – that is, if we hope to find some real solutions.

Chapter Eight

Keep Your Eyes on the Prize

Come now, and let us reason together. (Isaiah 1.18)

WHEN THE PHONE CALL came from Austin, Texas, I was surprised. Just two days after his election was secured in December 2000, President-elect Bush wanted a meeting with religious leaders to discuss faith-based initiatives in solving poverty. He was reaching beyond his base of conservative evangelicals. Would I come and suggest others who should be invited?

I was glad of the call because the subject was on my mind. While the American people and media had remained riveted to the presidential election, other news had fallen beneath the screen of national attention, including some alarming news about poor children and families.

So it seemed appropriate, just a few days before Christmas, to be sitting in a Sunday school classroom in Austin's First Baptist Church with a diverse group of religious leaders having a conversation with George W. Bush. Mr Bush listened and asked questions for over an hour, then stayed longer to mingle and talk to us individually. He said he believed in faith-based organizations (FBOs) and the important role they can play in solving social problems and wanted to make support for such efforts an important part of his administration.

George W. Bush asked us how to speak to the nation's soul. I suggested starting with our children, who embody our best hopes and reveal our worst failures as a society. We thanked him for being willing to include people in the meeting who hadn't supported his election and pledged to work with him *if* he chose to do something significant to reduce child poverty – fulfilling the promise made at the Republican National Convention to 'leave no child behind'.

We said that ideological warfare had allowed too many children to fall between the cracks of our faulty political discourse – liberal and conservative false choices about whether family values or living family incomes are more central to the causes and cures for poverty. I noted that churches across a broad spectrum are finding remarkable unity on these issues, and maybe it was time to try it on a political level. Evangelical and liberal, Catholic and Protestant, black and white church leaders have been convicted by prosperity's contradictions and united by the biblical imperatives of compassion and justice. Interfaith efforts have also greatly expanded. All around the country, faith-based initiatives to overcome poverty show remarkable progress. But presidential leadership is required, so the new president should send an early signal about poor children and families being high on his agenda.

Mr Bush asked theological questions of the religious leaders, like 'What is justice?' That is a key question, especially amid fears that an emphasis on faith-based initiatives will be used to substitute for crucial governmental responsibilities. We told him that in forging new partnerships to reduce poverty, the religious community will not only be service providers but also prophetic interrogators. Our vocation is to ask *why* people are poor, not just to care for the forgotten. Shelters and food banks aren't enough. We need solutions to the many problems of poverty, a pragmatic approach that produces results.

Could our divided political leaders come together around the moral cause of using our prosperity to finally address this nation's shamefully high poverty levels, especially among children? Could this divided nation find common ground if politicians would collaborate across old barriers as religious leaders have begun to do? Since neither party has succeeded in breaking the grip of persistent poverty, isn't a new bipartisan effort called for? Republicans preaching compassionate conservatism and family values, Democrats fighting for poor working families, and a religious community ready to lead by example and call the nation to its moral responsibilities could really do something significant about poverty.

All over the country, even where other efforts have failed, faith-based efforts are drawing national attention and making real progress on the most urgent social problems. Because of that, government officials are looking to partner with churches in new ways.

Thinking in new ways about the role of government in partnership with other institutions in the community is very important to success. In an article entitled 'Equal Partners: The Welfare Responsibility of Governments and Churches', Luis E. Lugo of the Pew Charitable Trusts sets forth some propositions that could help define the shape of new partnerships. Lugo says, 'The *first* is that the duty of solidarity requires a commitment to the poor from all those in society who are in a position to help. The *second* is that government's specific calling to do justice involves an important distributive role. The *third* is that government shares responsibility in this area with other institutions of civil society and that its primary task is to cooperate with these institutions so as to enable them to be of service to the poor. The *fourth* is that true reform demands going beyond devolving power from the national government to the states to a real empowerment of the institutions of civil society. The *fifth*, and final, proposition is that such cooperation between government and faith-based charities can fully honour the spirit of religious liberty embodied in the First Amendment to the United States Constitution.' No, government cannot and should not try to solve all our social problems. Yes, government still has vital responsibilities to provide a just and compassionate framework for society. The Catechism of the Catholic Church states that it is the responsibility of public authorities 'to make accessible to each what is needed to lead a truly human life: food, clothing, health, work, education and culture, suitable information, the right to establish a family, and so on'. It doesn't say that the government must provide all those things, but making sure they *are* provided is a duty of government.

But if faith-based organizations are indeed invited to the table, our role should not simply be to make government more efficient, but to make our country more just. It must not be only to 'clean up the mess' created by bad social policy or to take the place of legitimate government responsibilities, but to be a morally prophetic voice for new policies.

In this partnership, our job will be to raise the common moral values on which our society must build and to insist on a strong standard of the common good to guide public policy. We should argue that the development of public policy must not be dictated merely by the clash of power and competing interests but also by fundamental questions of right and wrong; it must be shaped by asking what our moral vision is, what kind of people we want to be, and what kind of country we want to have. For example, the national silence on the rapidly growing social inequality in America is stunning. That is a profoundly moral issue to which the faith community must speak as a biblical issue of justice.

Today there is an incredibly vibrant citizen politics occurring in many local communities. Much of it is tied to nonprofit institutions, among them, many faith-based organizations. National politics must wake up to that and begin to connect with all the grassroots energy and innovation. Perhaps we are at the beginning of that recognition as more and more political leaders are showing interest in the FBOs. We must learn how to make the connections between spirituality and politics, while vigorously protecting the First Amendment. There is enormous potential here, not just a few exemplary programmes, for a new vision of real social change.

As this book describes, denominations, congregations and faith-based organizations have provided services to their communities for years and have promoted linking the efforts of faith-based groups with government in ways that respect the First Amendment and the pluralism of a democratic society. It's often those grassroots groups that are closest to a community's problems – and they are often the ones that can develop the most successful solutions. Why not forge partnerships with the most effective non-profits, both religious and secular? And why discriminate against non-profits because they are religious?

I believe that a vibrant civil society, with major participation from the religious community, forging new partnerships with government, is an essential ingredient in overcoming poverty. I also believe that the resources to solve the problem simply don't exist sufficiently in civil society alone. Government, at all levels, must be involved. The real question is how government can most effectively help mobilize new multisector partnerships and target its resources in the most strategic way.

As to who should do what, there is a principle of Catholic social teaching that can help us here – it's called subsidiarity. 'Subsidiarity' means responsibilities and decisions should be attended to as closely as possible to the level of individual initiative in local communities and institutions. Remember

Chapter 6? Listen to those closest to the problem. Grassroots efforts, local organizations, families, churches, schools, local governments, small businesses, local unions and so forth, are often the best venue for problem solving. 'But', the same Catholic teaching says, 'larger government structures do have a role when greater social coordination and regulation are necessary for the common good.' Personally, I find the social teaching of the Catholic Church a rich resource in thinking through some of these complicated issues. Catholic social teaching is sometimes described as the best-kept secret in the Catholic Church! Nonetheless, I highly recommend it.

Perhaps the most helpful notion is the idea of the common good, which we have already discussed in relation to the epidemic of corporate mergers and layoffs in the late 1990s. The common good is a rich concept that can be applied to many areas of our social life and a unifying principle that can bring diverse people together. Listen to the wonderful definition of 'common good' in Catholic social teaching: 'the sum total of all those conditions of social living – economic, political, and cultural – which make it possible for women and men to readily and fully achieve the perfection of their humanity'. Now who is going to want to argue with that?

The clear message we must get across is that overcoming poverty, for example, is not the job of one sector or sphere; it is a shared responsibility. And working out that shared strategy is the work we have to do together. Try to avoid a view that concentrates all social activity in the government or the perspective that privatizes poverty and leaves it to the market and the charities. Instead, stress the responsibilities of the whole community, with each sector or institution acting out of its own best vocation. In each of our local communities, and at the level of national politics, we must insist that there are public commitments, safeguards, standards and allocations of resources that only government can accomplish or ensure. But at the same time, I believe that the vision and energy needed to overcome difficult social problems are frequently most available in what many have called the 'mediating institutions' of civil society – including churches, family, schools, small businesses, unions and a wide array of nonprofit organizations and voluntary associations. Why not use all our resources and institutions, and in the best possible combinations? That's the new partnership.

This pluralist approach to solving the problems of poverty could attract great support from concerned people across the political spectrum. Many now stress the importance of institutions that are intermediary between the individual and the state, while still affirming the crucial nature of government as a necessary countervailing force and protection against the otherwise unchecked power of large corporations in particular. These insights are not necessarily in conflict; they can work together. Neither a merely state-centred approach, nor a market-centred approach, nor a charity-centred approach is adequate to deal with the problem of poverty. A more promising direction is dynamic partnerships, linking the institutions of civil society, the government and the economic sector of businesses and unions.

The Role of Government

President Bush has said that faith-based organizations cannot 'replace' the role of government, which still has the responsibility for the large questions of Medicaid for poor children, health care for the uninsured, education and housing policy to name a few. With or without faith, grassroots efforts that save kids or rebuild neighbourhoods can't provide a social safety net for our whole society.

Whether the administration will keep that pledge will become evident in how its policies impact people in poverty. It will become clear in who most benefits from tax cuts, in the details of the federal budget, and in whether the crucial supports that low-income families need are included in the 2002 welfare reform reauthorization funding.

In the spring of 2001, I spoke at a large interfaith conference in Britain. The Labour government, led by Prime Minister Tony Blair, wanted to make a major new effort to partner with faith-based organizations. Blair delivered an excellent speech, taking clear government responsibility for budget and funding priorities that aim at overcoming poverty. But he also talked about the unique contribution faith-based organizations can make and invited them to be partners with the government.

Blair affirmed that, 'Community action has always been a central mission of the churches and other faith groups…And in carrying out this mission you have developed some of the most effective voluntary and community organizations in the country.'

He continued: 'It is misguided and outdated to suggest that there is a straight choice between voluntary activity and state activity. The two should go together. And where the two do go together – the government fully realizing its obligations, looking to the voluntary sector as partner not substitute – the impact is far greater than government acting on its own.' He went on to take responsibility for the government funding priorities that aim at overcoming poverty.

I also visited a faith-based organization called PECAN, located in a poor community in London. They participate in a government-funded job-training programme, called the New Deal, aimed at unemployed young adults. The government agencies that run the New Deal programme are often just offices where bureaucrats sit waiting for people to come in. When they do, they are handed 100 forms (that's right) to fill out. PECAN, on the other hand, sends their workers into the community, often knocking on doors in housing projects to find the people that need the job-training programme. They then help the young people fill out the confusing forms. And before the people come each day for their job training, the staff gathers to pray for each of them (on time not funded by the government). What the people get at PECAN is not proselytizing, but job training. Guess which programme works the best?

Britain is a very secular country, and talking about faith-based partnerships won't gain any politician many votes. They are talking about it because it works and actually helps people to escape poverty. Nobody in Britain wants government to fund religion – just results.

During my visit, I met with many government ministers, Members of Parliament, and lots of faith leaders from many different communities. Perhaps the best meeting I had was with Gordon Brown, the Chancellor of the Exchequer, who, as minister of the Treasury, is the second most powerful politician in Britain. Brown is the one who pushed the Jubilee 2000 campaign for debt reduction through the British government. His understanding of how faith-based partnerships could work for everybody's benefit made me want to move to Britain or, at least, send all our government leaders (from both parties) to London for some much needed education.

There is a progressive, democratic and pluralistic way to create faith-based partnerships that will really help to overcome poverty, as Mr Blair proposed. Liberals in America are making a foolish mistake by equating faith-based initiatives with right-wing politics and the Bush administration. And conservatives are make a hypocritical mistake in hoping faith-based initiatives might fulfil their dream of getting government out of social welfare programmes.

The potential of the faith-based initiative need not remain trapped in pro-Bush or anti-Bush politics. Many liberals so distrust President Bush and the Republican party's commitment to reducing poverty that they see the faith-based initiative as merely a deceptive way to shift the burdens of social welfare without the resources to carry it. And some conservatives support the faith-based initiative because they do see it as an alternative to significant public spending to reduce poverty and as a cover for tax cuts, while others are seeking to support their favourite religious ministries.

We must also be unswerving about the role and responsibility of government policies in providing the necessary resources to allow these programmes to realize their potential. Cutting spending on domestic programmes while expanding the role of faith-based service providers clearly will not work. But faith-inspired programmes and movements are becoming more and more crucial to social change worldwide. Such partnerships will be undertaken with governments across the political spectrum, and faith-based organizations must keep the pressure on all of them to put poor people on their political agenda.

The Conscience of the State

My most important question concerns the faith community's *prophetic voice*. Will partnership with the government mute or magnify the religious community's advocacy for social justice? My deepest concern is the prophetic integrity of religious groups who might appropriately receive some government funding. Why? Because those in power often prefer the service programmes of religious groups to their prophetic voice for social justice.

How can religious groups safeguard their prophetic integrity as they partner with government? That's far more important than the legal controversies. The biblical prophets held rulers, judges and employers accountable to the demands of justice. We should too. Faith communities must never become mere service providers; we are also called to be prophetic interrogators. Why do so many people remain poor in the midst of such amazing prosperity?

Dynamic new partnerships between faith-based groups and government are vitally needed, but they must not mute our prophetic voice. Faith-based groups that provide a social service must also be moral interrogators of the economic and political systems that make that service necessary in the first place. To prophetically challenge unjust structures and policies is part of our religious vocation, and we must not let potential government funding undermine it. Funding partnerships with government must not become a way for political leaders to buy off and silence religious leaders.

The Revd Martin Luther King, Jr, once said, 'The church must be reminded that it is not the master or the servant of the state, but rather the conscience of the state.' Practically, that means evaluating all government policies by how they impact poverty. Will people of faith challenge excessive tax cuts and budget priorities that benefit the wealthy and leave few resources to invest in effective anti-poverty strategies? Will we push for a health care policy that includes the 10 million children who are without coverage? Will we legislate for poor working families who need liveable incomes and affordable housing? When the time comes to reauthorize welfare reform, will we make sure to fund the critical elements that families need to move out of poverty's deadly cycle?

If words don't turn into deeds, then legislators, mayors, governors and presidents must hear the prophetic voice of faith-based organizations paraphrasing the prophet Amos: 'Take away from me your empty words, but let justice roll down like waters, and righteousness like an ever-flowing stream.'

I have no idea whether President Bush's faith-based initiative will ultimately turn out to be substantial or merely symbolic. But whether people trust the president or not, the faith-based initiative can be supported and used to raise the most important issues of biblical justice to the very administration that has proposed the initiative.

First, we should support faith-based and other community initiatives at the grassroots level precisely because they have such great potential to help children and families escape poverty.

Second, we should do it only in ways that keep social services and religious activities separate.

Third, we should insist on partnership between religious organizations and government, rather than replacement of one by the other, and not allow anybody to abdicate their responsibility. The role of government, especially in its budget priorities, is crucial.

Fourth, we should seize the moment as a prophetic opportunity, rather than just a danger. With all the attention on faith-based organizations, it may be the best time to speak the biblical language of both compassion and justice. While doing the work of compassion in neighbourhoods across the country, we can and must also make the demands of justice known to those in power.

That approach would begin to move us beyond Left and Right and, most important, would focus us all on the real goals of overcoming poverty for our poorest children. Let's discuss the real questions, but let's not allow our poorest children to be left behind in the wake of ideological arguments.

Chapter Nine

Tap the Power of Faith Communities

*Do not be conformed to this world, but be transformed
by the renewing of your minds. (Romans 12.2)*

THE UNITED STATES is a very religious country. We have always been
so and continue to be, despite the alleged secularization of
American society. The Pulitzer Prize-winning historian Garry Wills
says, 'Every time religiosity catches the attention of intellectuals, it
is as if a shooting star has appeared in the sky. One could hardly
guess, from this, that nothing has been more stable in our history,
nothing less budgeable, than religious belief and practice. Religion
does not shift or waver; the attention of the observers
does...Technology, urbanization, social mobility, universal
education, high living standards – all were supposed to eat away
at religion, in a wash of overlapping acids. But each has crested
over America, proving itself a solvent or a catalyst in other areas,
but showing little power to erode religion. The figures are
staggering. Poll after poll confirms them.'

The role of religion in American public life is a well-established
tradition, a deep influence in our culture and history.

Shifting Away from the Religious Right

Clearly, the religious Right has dominated the media's coverage on
religion and politics in the last two decades. But that is changing.
Perhaps the media have focused so much on the religious Right
because of its emphasis on electoral politics and gaining power
within the Republican party. The media's notoriously short
attention span is more suited to the wins and losses of elections
than to long-term efforts to turn neighbourhoods around. And

power is more interesting to the press than works of mercy and compassion.

The religious Right beat the Left to the punch in making the critical link between politics and moral values. But their agenda was too extreme and alarming to many, and they long ignored central biblical themes such as racial reconciliation and compassion for the poor. In the end, their too-close involvement in Republican party power-politics denied them the moral high ground that any movement toward a more spiritual politics needs.

But religious conservatives have done a much better job of focusing their message, engaging the media and building a national movement with local efforts than most of us doing faith-based on-the-ground social justice work have done. A cover story in the *Boston Globe* magazine was entitled 'One Nation Under God: How the Religious Right Changed the American Conversation'. And, indeed, it has. Even though I don't share many of their political conclusions, I am not one of those people who think that the religious Right has been an entirely negative force in American politics. The need for more value-centred politics, more support for families, more concern about the moral degradation of the popular culture and more emphasis on the value and dignity of human life are all positive concerns. The *Globe* article pointed out that even if one doesn't share their entire political agenda, one must admit that the religious Right has changed the conversation. Now, everyone is talking about their issues.

But it's hard to let go of old habits. Even though it's increasingly clear that the answers we need won't come from the Left or the Right alone, we continue to turn to one side or the other for solutions. The fact that even religious groups on both political sides tend to measure their success by marginal partisan political gains is especially disconcerting. Spiritually based social movements should measure their progress by concrete moral change and societal impact, not by adopting the false bottom lines of the pollsters and pundits. How can the election or defeat of a handful of members of Congress be viewed as a benchmark of victory either way, compared with monumental changes like the end of slavery or legal segregation led by religiously inspired abolitionist and civil rights movements of the past? Would the biblical prophets be satisfied with electoral body counts instead of the weightier matters of righteousness and justice?

Both the religious Right and the religious Left would do well to be more 'religious' and less political. Unfortunately, some religious people are still lining up on one or the other side of our all-too-polarized political battlefield. Some conservative religious leaders succumbed to the temptation to play the role of power brokers on the inside of Republican party battles for power and influence. And some liberal religious leaders just clamoured for photo opportunities at the Democratic White House.

Conservative religious activists have tried to take over the Republican party apparatus in local communities and turn out enough of their constituents to make them a real force in the party. They've certainly helped the Republican party win elections, but even some religious Right leaders are now openly questioning whether that has really served to advance a moral agenda. Meanwhile, on the other side, liberal religious activists bemoan the state of American politics and claim that the American people have been confused and duped by a highly energized religious and political right wing that has outspent, out-organized and outsmarted everybody else. They seem to assume that all the answers lie on the left side of the political spectrum, and they don't seem to question whether their dilemma is more than just tactical.

Isn't it about time to admit that neither liberal nor conservative solutions have been working very well, and that we need some new directions? That's what many people in America believe; I've heard it all across the country.

Conservatives have been right about many things: the importance of a values-based politics, personal responsibility, and strong families, and the dangers of bureaucracy to healthy citizenship. But conservatives have been wrong with respect to racism and their failure to defend the poor. Conservatives have been guilty of a double standard in attacking big government while uncritically championing both corporate power and militarism. And on the edges of conservatism, a legitimate pro-life commitment has been turned, by a zealous few, into an abusive and sometimes murderous crusade against the women and medical personnel at abortion clinics. Conservatives could learn much from the rich traditions of nonviolent movements in their efforts to change the nation's attitudes toward abortion. And some conservatives have also allowed their pro-family values to become obsessively focused on campaigns against the civil rights of homosexuals, who are irrationally and unfairly blamed for the very real breakdown of family life in America.

Liberals have been right in fighting for racial, economic and gender justice, in protecting the environment, and in standing for peace. But the liberal Left has too often failed to uphold critical personal and cultural values, such as strong family life, and has instead offered the nation a litany of moral relativism. For example, many now believe we must stop talking about giving 14-year-olds the information and tools to make their own decisions about whether to have sex. Instead, we are told we must create a moral environment around adolescents that persuades them that sexual activity at their age is a bad choice. Teaching young people both healthy sexual behaviour and just racial behaviour is essential to their learning positive values. Finally, liberalism has made a fundamental mistake in seeing a woman's right to choose as the only moral issue at stake in the abortion dilemma.

Both conservatives and liberals have often forgotten their best and original impulses while becoming tied to vested interests. Most conservatives can't seem to challenge the behaviour of big corporations, even when they are trampling on the most sacred of traditional family and moral values. Similarly, many liberals never dare to challenge teachers' and public employees' unions or government bureaucracies, even when they protect only their own interest, rather than those of the people they are supposed to serve.

Conservatives have been too uncritical of Wall Street, and liberals have relied too much on state solutions to our social problems. On the Right, the market is the magical solution to every social problem. On the Left, societal responsibilities have often been simply equated with governmental ones. What government can and must do, what the social responsibilities of corporations are, and what other civil institutions can best contribute are critical issues for both liberals and conservatives.

The new discussions we need require a values-based approach, instead of just taking sides. Making a moral impact upon a society usually requires subjecting politics to outside moral criteria, rather than merely playing the inside power games. Holding politics accountable is best accomplished by independent social movements with clear moral priorities. And that demands more than just seeking a place at the table of political power.

But the conversation about religion and public life appears to be changing again. Today, new findings point to the potential for renewing religion's role in seeking social justice. First, a recent survey shows that 86 per cent of the American people (religious or not) believe that 'churches and religious organizations should spend more time helping the poor'. When churches show little concern for the poor, this is perceived as a big gap in their integrity, say more and more people. The general public consistently view Jesus as being on the side of the poor and oppressed, and the hunger for making that connection back to Jesus and restoring the churches' social justice leadership is now evident in many places.

Second, it used to be that grassroots community organizing around the country was led by political parties, clubs and labour unions committed to economic justice. But the nature of community organizing has fundamentally changed, and today most of it is being done through the churches. It takes several forms, but most of the nation's largest community-organizing networks have now chosen the churches and local congregations as their primary organizing base and constituency. Several other community- and economic-development networks are explicitly Christian. Then there are all the other social ministries carried out by the churches and congregations in every community across the country.

Another discussion is making its way into the public arena through the religious community. It's the moral conversation about poverty, racism and the growing economic inequality in America. New religious voices are beginning to be heard and are attracting public attention, and it is possible to see how the religious community might now impact the national debate on these issues of social justice. As Fred Clark, a young organizer from Evangelicals for Social Action, said at a Call to Renewal town meeting, 'We must look forward to the day when the politicians feel they have to "pacify" the churches on the issue of poor people, just like they have tried to do on other issues.' When the *New Yorker*, *George*, the *New York Times* and even *Worth* magazine all focus on the connection between spirituality and politics and faith-based solutions to social problems, something new is in the air. In addition, a whole series of essays in scholarly and social policy journals have appeared, showing the positive results of faith-based initiatives. The articles have been very interesting indeed, with reporters who normally deal with secular issues struggling to understand something that they recognize has

growing social and political significance. It's the first time in
several years that media coverage of religion's role has not even
mentioned the religious Right. They are not part of this story.

Joe Klein, in a *New Yorker* article called 'In God They Trust',
described the dramatic reduction in youth crime in Boston we've
already discussed, and how 'unconditional love' is an effective
programme to save kids from the ravages of drugs, violence and
poverty. Naomi Wolf, writing in *George*, said that the 'blend of
compassionate political action and spiritual rhetoric' is the right
combination to mobilize people in a new political direction. She
said, 'This newly energized movement...may well be the
winning centre of American politics of the near future.'

John DiIulio is convinced that a 'God-centred and problem-
centred approach' will provide the most successful strategy. He
believes that the right-wing political agenda of groups such as the
Christian Coalition won't ultimately speak to the place where most
Christians and most other Americans really are now. Rather, a new
agenda that is neither Left nor Right, which combines personal
responsibility and moral values with a frontal assault on racism
and poverty, will be increasingly successful.

But what are the alternatives to the old political labels? And
what does it mean to go beyond Right and Left? We certainly don't
want to settle for a mushy middle. Searching for common ground
is not the same thing as becoming a political centrist. Don't do the
trendy thing of grabbing the political centre; instead, search for
the moral centre of an issue or a public debate. Find common
ground by seeking higher ground, and you'll discover a whole
group of new and unexpected allies.

A new value-based politics could be moral without being
sectarian. Most of us still probably think about predicting the future
when we hear the word 'prophetic', but its meaning in religious
traditions has more to do with a social critique willing to raise the
moral questions of justice that most ignore. Drawn from the more
prophetic elements of our social, political, spiritual and religious
traditions, a new politics would identify common moral values on
which to build. It would seek to articulate a moral vision of politics
that is neither Left nor Right, but draws on the strengths of each side,
learns from their mistakes, and transcends both with new solutions.
A fresh discussion of values – both personal and social – is
paramount in forging a new and prophetic vision that is morally
rooted but not ideologically compartmentalized. A prophetic politics

wouldn't hesitate to be courageous in its pronouncements and would seek to avoid being tied to predictable special interests. And it would insist on a strong standard of the common good to guide public policy. New political visions shouldn't be restricted to discussions of government policy but should also include conversations about the cultural and moral assumptions that are the unspoken underpinnings of our public discourse. For example, how does the influence of materialism fundamentally shape our political discussions? Rabbi Michael Lerner has critiqued the empty ethics of selfish individualism and offered instead a 'politics of meaning'. We might also ask how a more consistent regard for human rights, wherever they are violated, could challenge both ideological camps. A politics of values would raise the deeper questions that both the Right and the Left often leave out.

Rather than the old language of 'the centre' or 'the middle', the challenge of building new common ground may be a better way to describe the quest for a value-based politics that is neither Left nor Right. In every region of the nation, the effort to build that common ground is being widely affirmed. All of these efforts are really ways of speaking about the need to rebuild our civil society, which has crumbled so badly. It is finally all about the politics of community, and that could become attractive to a whole range of people.

America today is a pluralistic society, one composed of many faiths and spiritual interests. Any new social agenda must work within this increasingly diverse culture. Ron Thiemann, a Lutheran theologian at the Harvard Divinity School, insightfully points out that religious pluralism, not secularism, is the greater challenge ahead in American life. A growing interest in spirituality has disproved and confounded the advocates of secularism. But that interest takes many shapes today. There is much going on in American religion beyond the churches. An increasingly lively Jewish Renewal movement is evidencing both an inviting spirituality and social commitment, which attracts many who have been repelled by organized religion. There are 4.1 million Muslims in America today, more than the number of either Presbyterians or Episcopalians and, soon, more than the number of Jews. There are also 2.4 million Buddhists and 1 million Hindus, and both religions are growing.

To navigate such diversity, both absolutism and relativism are inadequate, says Thiemann. The best way forward may be a 'pilgrim discipleship', and by this he means being committed to the truths of one's own belief but open to the fresh insights of others. He names four characteristics of a pilgrim discipleship: God is a transcendent mystery; out of death comes life; true religion shows itself in ministry to outcasts; and be prepared for the unexpected. Finding God in unexpected places, while maintaining a strong commitment to one's own faith, opens one up to others and leaves no room for arrogance, only humility.

Many people today are more comfortable with 'spiritual' rather than 'religious' values. But religious or spiritual experience reveals what the spiritual dimension has the power to do and why it must be at the centre of any efforts to change our communities.

Radical Religion

I walked through the historic Holy Trinity church on Clapham Common, in south London. This Anglican parish was the home church to William Wilberforce, the abolitionist English Parliamentarian who wrote Britain's anti-slave trade legislation. Wilberforce, and a group of Christian laymen called the Clapham Sect, were behind much of the social reform that swept Britain in the late eighteenth and early nineteenth centuries. The current vicar was very proud to show me round. On the wall were pictures of these typically English-looking gentlemen who helped to turn their country upside down. Other such memorabilia abound in the beautiful old church, now perched on the edge of the rich green expanse of urban park that the British call a common.

The vicar specifically pointed to an old, well-worn table. 'This is the table upon which William Wilberforce wrote the anti-slavery act', he said proudly. 'We now use this table every Sunday for communion.' I was struck – here, in dramatic liturgical symbol, the secular and the sacred are brought together with powerful historical force. How did we ever separate them? What became of religion that believed its duty was to change its society on behalf of justice?

William Wilberforce was a convert of the religious revivals that transformed eighteenth-century England. His life and his vocation as a Member of Parliament profoundly changed by his newfound faith, Wilberforce became a force for moral politics. His mentor, John Newton, had helped sail a slave ship before he was converted, then turned against slavery and became well known for writing the well-loved hymn 'Amazing Grace'. Newton's immortal words, 'Amazing Grace, how sweet the sound, that saved a wretch like me', spoke not merely of private guilt and piety, but of having turned from being a slave trader who trafficked in human flesh to being a religious leader who helped lead the battle against slavery. His conversion produced a social and political transformation as well as a personal one.

The same became true of Wilberforce, who first heard Newton speak when he was young but regarded his real conversion as resulting from a conversation with his mentor in 1786. Two years later Wilberforce introduced his first anti-slave trade motion into Parliament. It was defeated, and would be defeated nine more times until it passed in 1807. It was a historic and moral victory, but Wilberforce wouldn't be satisfied until slavery was abolished altogether. He tirelessly worked toward that goal, year after year. Finally, in 1833, Parliament passed a Bill abolishing slavery, and Wilberforce died three days later, his work finally done. Wilberforce's life is a testament to the power of conversion and the persistence of faith.

Similarly, in nineteenth-century America, religious revivalism was linked directly with the abolition of slavery and movements of social reform. Christians helped lead the abolitionist struggle, efforts to end child labour, projects to aid working people and establish unions, and even the battle to obtain voting rights for women. Here were evangelical Christians fighting for social causes, an activity that evangelicals are hardly associated with today. Nineteenth-century evangelist Charles Finney, the Billy Graham of his day, didn't shy away from identifying the gospel with the anti-slavery cause. He was a revivalist and also an abolitionist. For him, the two went together. Finney is said to have invented the 'altar call', well known to us today in gatherings like the Billy Graham crusades, where people are invited to get up out of their seats and come down to the front of the pulpit to profess their new faith. Finney invited people down the aisle too, but his motivations are reported to have been very pragmatic also. He wanted the names of his converts in order to sign them up for the abolitionist cause. He was an organizer as well as an evangelist. And he had an agenda.

The Big Split

So what happened to Christianity in the twentieth century? Put simply, there was a big split. American Protestantism split into two camps in the early 1900s. The schism went deep and remained a permanent divide throughout the rest of the century. The fundamentalists took the conservative road of personal piety and correct doctrine, while the modernists chose the liberal path of the social gospel. And the two choices were conceived by most as mutually exclusive. One group would come to be called evangelical and the other liberal.

Both fundamentalist and liberal Protestants questioned whether the large numbers of Catholic immigrants arriving in America in the twentieth century were really Christians – their Catholic religion would not be accepted. And most white churches of all denominations wished to keep segregated from their black Christian brothers and sisters, who started their own churches.

Thus four basic constituencies of American Christianity remained apart through most of the twentieth century: evangelical, mainline Protestant, Catholic and the historic black churches. Each developed its own Christian culture and world, complete with schools, other institutions, language, traditions, networks of relationships, agendas, priorities and, of course, opinions about the other groups.

I was brought up in the evangelical world ('evangelical' generally replaced 'fundamentalist' after World War II). Our small Plymouth Brethren Assembly in Detroit, Michigan, saw itself as a direct descendant of biblical Christianity and the early church. We looked upon other evangelical churches favourably, as long as they 'preached the gospel'. The Baptists and independent Bible churches were closest to us. But most of the mainline liberal Protestant denominations were deeply suspect theologically, and all Catholics were targets of our evangelism because we thought they worshipped Mary and the pope rather than God. Nobody ever talked about the black churches; it was as if they didn't exist.

Later I discovered that Catholics learned similar prejudices about us Protestants as they were growing up, and that liberal Protestants regarded most evangelicals as unsophisticated, uneducated, and unpleasant. No matter where they lived, evangelicals were seen as Bible-thumping street preachers who might corner you and ask, probably in a Southern accent, if you were saved. Interestingly, black Christians didn't perceive great differences among the warring white church factions, at least so far as racism toward them was concerned, which seemed to be the one thing most white Christians had in common.

Twentieth-Century Ecumenism

If we are to successfully tap the power of faith communities, we have to understand them. A little history of the churches' divisions may help those working for social change – whether they themselves are religious or not – who want to collaborate with the churches. 'Ecumenism', or the effort on the part of churches to get together in the twentieth century, never broke down the divisions I've described above. In fact, the modern ecumenical movement has occurred almost solely among mainstream Protestant churches. The formation of the Federal Council of the Churches of Christ in America and various church councils in Europe at the beginning of the twentieth century launched the collaboration of the leading Protestant denominations. Later, consolidations into the National Council of Churches (NCC) in 1950 and the World Council of Churches (WCC) in 1948 completed the task. But again, many churches and groups were left out. It is significant to note that the principal reasons for coming together had to do with missions and service. 'Doctrine divides but service unites' became an early motto whose spirit was key to future, wider, ecumenical realities.

With the formation of these councils, Presbyterians and Methodists, Episcopalians and Congregationalists, Lutherans and some Baptists, among others, came together for at least some common goals. And some of the results were, indeed, impressive – for instance, the leadership the National Council of Churches offered in the American civil rights movement and the role of the World Council of Churches in helping to end apartheid in South Africa. However, efforts to agree on theological issues and matters of church order and polity were usually much more problematic than joint efforts on common social agendas.

Evangelical Christians were rarely at the ecumenical table – both by choice and by exclusion. In fact, the ecumenical table has belonged to liberal Protestants, who have been adamant gatekeepers. Consequently, evangelicals formed their own networks, such as the National Association of Evangelicals, founded in 1942; established a myriad of para-church organizations for mission; spawned great student movements such as Inter-Varsity Christian Fellowship and Campus Crusade for Christ; and conducted joint evangelistic efforts, most notably the Billy Graham crusades, which even made common cause with mainline Protestant and Catholic churches.

Within the two Protestant camps, scores of organizations and associations were produced. Both liberal and evangelical groups founded their own colleges, institutions and publications. Evangelical pastors read *Christianity Today*, founded by Billy Graham, while their liberal Protestant counterparts read the *Christian Century* or *Christianity & Crisis*, the latter founded by the eminent theologian Reinhold Niebuhr.

All along, Catholics have pursued their own course, evolving from a marginalized church, full of many new immigrants, to a major cultural and political force by the end of the twentieth century. They, too, generally, have not been at the ecumenical table of liberal Protestants and, like the evangelicals, developed a whole network of schools and other institutions that made a deep impact in local communities around the country. Catholics actually have become a bridge constituency in American church life, espousing much of the cultural conservatism embraced by evangelicals as well as the social conscience shared by liberal Protestants, particularly in relationship to the poor. Catholic bishops could find themselves outside the White House protesting partial-birth abortions one day and the signing of a draconian welfare Bill the next.

The black churches in America have defied the polarization between white liberals and conservatives by consistently prioritizing both spiritual conversion and social justice. In spite of having their own divisions, the biblical balance of personal piety and public prophecy for justice has remained strong in most black congregations of all denominations, while their white counterparts created a century of false choices. The black churches in the South and around the country led and became the moral infrastructure of the civil rights movement – the greatest ecumenical moment of the twentieth century. Nevertheless, black Christians were still not given a real place and voice at ecumenical tables controlled by white Christians for most of the century. As we go into the twenty-first century, that finally has begun to change.

Beyond the evangelicals, mainline Protestants, Catholics and black churches, perhaps the greatest uncharted religious movement of the century was the Pentecostal and charismatic revivals, which emphasized direct personal experience of the Holy Spirit and very lively expressions of worship. Though treated with suspicion by all the other church groups, Pentecostals are the fastest-growing sector in the worldwide church at the beginning of the twenty-first century. While their appeal crosses all denominational, racial and even class lines, twentieth-century Pentecostals and charismatics became another group unto themselves, often distrusting those who didn't share their litmus tests of what it means to be 'filled by the Holy Spirit'.

The other constituency that doesn't fit neatly within the boundaries of the four groups is the Orthodox churches. These are the congregations from the Eastern Christian world, whose blend of deep worship, powerful liturgy and personal piety offers a different perspective in Western ecumenical debates.

The Twenty-First Century Church

But the prospects for churches coming together and playing a more helpful social leadership role are much brighter now. Understanding the changes now going on will help anyone who wants to work with the churches.

The church of the twenty-first century will eventually look quite different from the church today. Yes, there will be a church, despite the dire predictions of many who keep pointing to declining church rolls and influence among the mainline Protestants. There may even be more churches and more people going to them than we see today. But the churches themselves will be different, and the relationships among them will consequently be changing.

The best way to describe how the churches have been operating is likening them to *vertical* silos – tall, narrow structures into which ideas and leadership are dropped from the top, in the hope that they will reach down to the grassroots level. But the vertical style of organization and leadership that has characterized most churches is already changing. In the future, *horizontal* patterns of relationship between congregations will be the normative style, and those ecclesial interconnections will go beyond denominations to cross the lines that have divided us for a century.

These new connections are profoundly local and focused on cooperation around specific and practical issues facing communities and neighbourhoods. Three factors are producing the new horizontal configuration: a cultural crisis of values, a deep spiritual hunger that transcends old ideological and religious categories, and a more recognized social role for churches. Together, these forces will call forth a new ecumenical reality. The vertical constituencies of the twentieth-century American churches will come together horizontally for twenty-first-century projects and endeavours. Indeed, it is already happening.

In the final quarter of the twentieth century, the rigid patterns of American church life began to change. The civil rights movement and the war in Vietnam impacted a new generation of evangelicals. They discovered the forgotten evangelical movements of the nineteenth century, whose strong social conscience focused on abolitionism, concern for the poor and the equality of women. They began to meet children of mainline Protestantism who were also hungry for a more personal spirituality and a deeper grounding in biblical faith. Catholics, taking permission from Vatican II, also rediscovered the Bible and embarked on a spiritual pilgrimage of personal and parish renewal, but with a social conscience that twentieth-century evangelicalism lacked. Black congregations grew within the predominantly white denominations, soon to be followed by their Latino and Asian brothers and sisters. Pentecostal pastors in storefront churches began to look outward.

The real ecumenism of the last 25 years has taken place in soup kitchens and homeless shelters more than at tables of theologians trying to find unity on the meaning of the Eucharist. Instead, Methodists, Baptists, Mennonites and Catholics have been sharing bread together at nuclear test sites, outside the White House or the South African embassy, and in the jail cells to which they were taken after their spiritual protests.

I remember the May 1985 events that Sojourners sponsored around the Christian holiday of Pentecost in Washington, DC. Christians from around the country conducted nonviolent civil disobedience at symbolic sites around the city to register their moral conscience regarding many issues that cut across traditional political lines: budget cuts against the poor, the superpowers' deployment of first-strike nuclear weapons, the American wars in Central America, the Soviet invasion of Afghanistan, and the nation's acceptance of 1.5 million abortions every year.

We soon had the DC jail full of Christians – hundreds of them singing and praying through most of the night. The jail acoustics seemed favourable and we sounded pretty good. By the end of the night, the jailhouse choir was taking requests from the guards to sing their favourite hymns! Baptist and Benedictine choir directors, evangelical pastors and Franciscan priests, Presbyterian theologians and Maryknoll sisters, and lay people from virtually every denomination spent the night in jail, not only singing, but talking with one another.

'The whole church is here', exclaimed an exuberant clergyman. 'I must be in heaven', smiled a Catholic sister as she woke up to the strains of 'Amazing Grace', coming from the men's side of the jail. And one seminarian, who had slept all night on the concrete floor, said he would have paid money to be there for the best theological education he'd had so far.

Spiritual Formation

It's not only social action that is bringing people together, but also their spiritual hunger. Catholic spiritual programmes that focus on personal and parish renewal have grown around the country. Evangelical Bible studies have proliferated across the nation, involving people of every and no denomination. And prayer circles of support can be found now in virtually every workplace, including the halls of Congress. When Christians pray and study the Bible together, they also talk and come to know and support one another across all the former dividing lines.

As our culture's values continue to disintegrate, centres of positive values and activities will draw more and more people. Instead of just complaining and blaming others, church congregations could become the places where moral reconstruction begins, if they are ready to rise to the challenge. Within the nurturing bonds that churches provide, broken families can be supported and many put back together again; children can find role models and moral guidance to navigate dangerous cultural waters; employers can be motivated to serve the common good, not just the bottom line; and young people can learn the deeper rewards of service compared with the numbing drive of materialism.

Churches, not just New Age seminars, could respond directly to the obvious spiritual hunger across the land and be less afraid of its excesses. Congregations can become the much needed places of spiritual formation that our society desperately lacks, stressing character over success, spirituality over consumption, fidelity over gratification, honesty over expediency, leadership over celebrity, and integrity over everything else. Limitless technology, endless consumption and never-ending work have clearly not answered the longings of the human heart. The spiritual hunger at the beginning of the twenty-first century is even greater than at the beginning of the twentieth, and the churches still have the best opportunity to respond.

In order to respond to that spiritual hunger, the churches need to turn their present divisions into resources for renewal. Virtually every denomination began with an impulse for reform, an insight that was unique, or a truth that helped define it. Each therefore has, within its own history, a tradition of renewal. Yet most of those renewing impulses have long since been forgotten, and the traditions have simply turned into divisions.

The transforming power of the early church is still embedded in the traditions of every congregation today. The renewing power of every Catholic religious order or Protestant denomination is available to be appropriated anew. Indeed, the Catholic orders are all learning that the road to renewal begins with a return to the earliest 'charisms' – the founding ideas or purposes that created the community – and then with the application of those charisms to the contemporary world.

Increasingly, American Protestants choose their churches with little reference to denomination. Other factors are more important: neighbourhood location, Sunday school and youth activities, stimulating preaching and worship, and community service. Some might call that a reflection of the wider society's consumer mentality, but it also reflects a desire to relate church in more meaningful ways to families and local communities. In fact, many families are turning to independent community churches, which are now the fastest-growing segment in the country. Most Catholics still select a parish for Mass but are more and more involved with Protestants in everything from social ministry to Bible study and prayer. And younger evangelicals are far less fearful than their parents were of mixing with both Catholics and other Protestants. Black Christians still understand the central role of the black church in their communities but now can be found partnering with white congregations for the sake of inner-city ministry and racial reconciliation.

Drinking from Other Wells

The denominational ties and loyalties that Christians feel today are weaker than ever. And never before have Christians been more interested in traditions other than their own. Many people find themselves drinking from wells of spirituality far afield from where they began. Catholic retreat centres are overflowing with Protestants. Lively evangelical services draw crowds of hungry worshippers from every denomination. And few can fire the souls of American Christians, regardless of their racial and cultural identity, more than a black preacher or choir. When church-led efforts to meet the social needs of the community have opened up in urban churches, they have drawn volunteers from every kind of church and others from no church at all.

We can see the possibilities of churches and denominations turning their divisions into the spiritual wells of tradition from which we all drink. Important theology can be found in virtually every church tradition, and it should not simply be amalgamated into a new ecumenism. In other words, ecumenism for the twenty-first century should not be viewed as a bland, common-denominator Christianity. Rather, it should emerge from the exciting rediscovery of the strength of each of our traditions, which are seen as gifts to be offered instead of walls to divide.

That could produce wonderful results. We all could recover the wonderful Catholic sense of God's presence in all of life and the world, and regain a commitment on the part of every church to take spiritual responsibility for the life of the parish in which it finds itself. The depth and quality of Catholic social teaching also offer much to Protestants who are looking to move beyond the old categories of Left and Right, and the spiritual formation available from Catholic religious communities could be a powerful resource for the whole of the church.

The evangelical invitation of a personal relationship with Jesus could bring people back to the churches, where membership has been steadily declining. The spiritual energy and passion of evangelical churches are desperately needed today in churches where both are in short supply. If Bible study and prayer again become mainstays of Christian life, small groups doing both would draw spiritually hungry people who are not inclined to venture into a more formal church service.

Mainline Protestant churches could rediscover the best of their own social gospel tradition, which refused to separate personal piety from social action. Instead of backing off from strong social commitments because of declining numbers, the major denominational churches could strengthen their prophetic social witness by renewing their call to evangelism. And the exemplary commitments of many mainline Protestant denominational churches to the gifts and leadership of women could offer much to many Catholic, evangelical and black churches whose patterns are still quite patriarchal.

Both evangelical and mainline Protestant churches could recover their historical roots in the revival traditions and in the reformed traditions from which they come. The revivalist movements swept across nineteenth-century America, making converts and challenging the social evils of the day. The Reformed tradition refused to divide life into sacred and secular, private and public, and insisted that everything must be brought under the Lordship of Jesus Christ.

The Anabaptist tradition, which created the Historic Peace Churches of Mennonites, Brethren and Quakers, could teach the contemporary world about the limits of military force in resolving conflicts. Their strong witness for nonviolence, peacemaking and simple living could speak to a great hunger today from both the religious and the nonreligious.

White Christians could finally look to their black brothers and sisters for instruction in how to feed hungry souls and bodies. The spiritual power and social courage of the black churches have provided the best single contribution of American Christianity to the worldwide church. It is time for that contribution to be fully accepted at home.

The great influx of Latino and Asian Christians to the United States is further transforming the churches, and the emergence of Native American congregations offers to diversify the face of American Christianity even more. All of these should be allowed to express their own indigenous spiritualities.

As the traditions that divide become the resources that renew, we will see the emergence of a new ecumenical table in every community. Old ecumenical structures must give way to new ecumenical networks. The mainline Protestants who controlled the old table are vitally needed at the new one, but it is no longer their table; in fact, no one needs to control it.

The Protestant denominations of the World Council of Churches and the National Council of Churches seem to be recognizing this new reality and are making attempts to reach out to other families of churches. Catholics and evangelicals are finding they have more and more in common as well, and both seem willing to sit down with their mainline Protestant neighbours. Some white Christians finally understand how much they need their black and brown brothers and sisters, especially in a society desperate for models of racial repentance and reconciliation.

This new table of Christian unity is possible only as we seek to find the common ground that has been hidden by our divisions. If we don't, a new period of division awaits us, perhaps not along denominational and constituency lines but along social and cultural cleavages. Instead of helping to resolve society's deepest conflicts, the church would probably ratify them. How tragic if the future church were simply defined by pro-gay and anti-gay congregations, pro-choice and pro-life partisans, and conservative and liberal voting blocs. It's a future we can avoid, but only if we let our theological vision and spiritual clarity – rather than political positions – define our public witness.

Every large-scale Christian project and endeavour must strive to bring all the church families together. On many community issues, we must learn to sit down with brothers and sisters from other faith traditions. We have yet to determine the shape of a new interfaith collaboration that moves beyond highly unsatisfying lowest-common-denominator worship services to real partnership, where everyone is free to be and bring who they are. But that is already beginning too. I've seen it all around the country.

Instead of a church made up of divided kingdoms and warring factions, the church of the twenty-first century could well become a rich mosaic of interconnected faith communities. Nothing would be better news for a society looking for social leadership, cultural healing and spiritual grounding.

The 'Body of Christ'

That twenty-first-century church can already be found. I was teaching week-long courses in western Canada and in the American Southwest. Both were titled 'Who Speaks for God?' and both included clergy and lay leaders from across the whole theological and denominational spectrum. We had 27-year-olds and 87-year-olds, pastors, professors, doctors, nurses, lawyers, union members, community organizers, business people, economists, directors of homeless shelters, computer programmers, school teachers, retired people, students, mothers and fathers, longserving activists and new explorers.

A recurring theme in both classes was the hunger for new 'dialogue', for 'bridge building', and for new relationships across former dividing lines. Once again I saw how weary people have become of the old liberal/conservative debates that have turned the churches against each other. Class members came from all of the old sides, but shared a community of sorts for the week in residential settings and discovered that they really did have more in common as Christians than their various churches had been able to find.

Growing unity on the problem of poverty was evident throughout the week, and the prospect of forming new partnerships back home in their local communities was particularly exciting to many. But we didn't shy away from the hot topics either. We also talked about abortion, family values and homosexuality. After a whole morning session on abortion in Canada (where the issue is also very divisive and controversial), one of the clergy in the class remarked, 'I've never been in a better conversation on abortion. Nobody walked out, and people didn't even start yelling at each other. We all listened for a change. It was really amazing.'

Both the sanctity of human life and the rights of women were affirmed. Through discussion, people on different sides of issues found it possible to agree on the importance of traditional two-parent families for raising children without scapegoating single mothers or blaming homosexuals for the breakdown of heterosexual families. And both the Right and the Left got criticized for trying to divide the church over issues such as these. People were tired of the extremes controlling the debate on many issues, and were looking for some common ground without compromising their convictions.

But in addition to finding common ground, there was a real enjoyment of the diversity of the faith community. When we can stop fighting for a moment, we begin to realize the richness of the many traditions and experiences that are the church. Young Christians were clearly marvelling at the wisdom and faith of those much older. Pastors across denominational lines began openly sharing their joys and their struggles and praying for one another. We both laughed and cried together, rejoicing together over new marriages and babies and sorrowing together over circumstances of sickness, loneliness and loss. Several people began to talk about 'the body of Christ', a traditional term for the church, and the oldest member of the New Mexico course exclaimed on the last day of class, 'We should get together next year. I think we're a great group!' Addresses, phone numbers and e-mails were eagerly exchanged, and many expressed the extra support they will now feel just knowing that 'you all are out there'. Some suggested we were parting like teenagers leaving friends behind after summer camp. Not only was it a lot of fun, but it again proved to me that our divisions can be overcome.

Perhaps it is easier in a beautiful summer setting for a week with normal responsibilities left behind. But I wondered how church people could begin to experience some of that same depth of sharing and community across the normal boundaries of our lives. Christian unity does not come easily, and it must never come at the expense of gospel truth. But all too often, in the name of our truths, we have just been attacking one another in the churches, and a disbelieving world sees no reason to join us. Remember how Jesus said the world will know we are Christians? 'That you have love one for another' was not a commandment to be easily set aside because of honest disagreements among Christians. It was that love which Jesus called us to, and two groups of Christians got to experience it, in the lush forests of British Columbia and in the spectacular desert of northern New Mexico. It was enough to make you fall in love with the church again and gave me a very exciting glimpse of the twenty-first-century church.

A New Social Role: Why Faith Communities Will Lead

As well as responding to the crisis of values and society's spiritual hunger, faith-based groups have an advantage over many other institutions when it comes to the kind of community organizing and development most needed today. It finally comes down to the question of social leadership – who is best situated to offer critical components like vision, direction, credibility, longevity, trust and, of course, organizable constituencies. Faith communities may be in the best position to lead efforts for social renewal because of their inherent characteristics and commitments, enabling them to be community conveners in broad-based efforts involving many different kinds of organizations. There are three sets of

essential ingredients that are at the heart of why it is so critical
to tap the power of faith communities.

Message and Motivation

In a society where market values increasingly predominate, faith
communities can offer a sense of meaning, purpose and moral
value that is increasingly missing in the society. When people feel
reduced to mere consumers and life is reduced to shopping, faith
communities can speak directly to the deep spiritual hunger that so
many people experience. In the community of faith, persons are
more than marketing data for advertisers or polling data for
politicians; they are the children of God with immense and sacred
value, created in the very image of God.

Faith communities are also best situated to speak to society's
moral and spiritual impoverishment, which others seem to accept
as inevitable. They can help to re-establish a sense of ethics and
values. The faith community makes it possible to do more than
look out for number one. Faith communities offer people practical
opportunities to love their neighbour, serve their community,
contribute to a larger purpose and sacrifice for something worth
believing in. In the faith community, the values of compassion,
community and solidarity have a theological foundation, not merely
a sentimental one. Hope is more than an optimistic feeling; it is a
firm conclusion drawn from trusting the promises of God.

The values you need for organizing are rooted in the very essence
of the faith community. Eugene Rivers, pastor of the Azuza Christian
Community in Boston, says that 'only the church has the moral
authority and the vocabulary to introduce transcendent concepts of
personal worth and the sacredness of life that will both inspire
responsibility on a personal level and introduce purpose and
definition to the role of civil government on a societal level'. Thus,
faith can be used to undergird, legitimize and inspire social action.

Counterculture and Prophetic Voice

Faith communities are intended to be distinct communities,
with ethics distinct from those of the surrounding society. The
apostle Paul writing to the Romans says, 'Do not be conformed
to this world, but be transformed by the renewing of your
minds.' Alternative visions arise from alternative communities.

Such communities can become support bases for nurturing and training, networking and mobilizing. The symbols and rituals of the faith community can become powerful educators and mobilizers for committed and even risky action. For example, black churches in the South constituted a coherent subculture in the midst of a white-dominated society. As such they reminded their members who they really were and what they could really do. Churches became the practical place to organize car pools to sustain a bus boycott and the spiritual place to prepare oneself for nonviolent confrontation with police truncheons and dogs.

A countercultural community can have a prophetic public voice. Here is where the authority and trust that religious communities often enjoy in our society can be utilized for the common good. Who will tell the truth, or even try to find it, when falsehoods prevail? Who will stand up for those who are being left out and behind, or whose human rights are being violated? Who will question the easy and hedonistic assumptions of the popular culture? Who will challenge the government's authority when it becomes violent and abusive? Why did the government of El Salvador assassinate Archbishop Oscar Romero? They were afraid of his authority in challenging their political repression. And as a slain martyr, Romero gained even more authority. The faith community has the moral authority to make justice a priority.

Institution and Constituency

The most common institutions in local communities are the churches and the schools – and the churches are in much better shape than the schools. Churches have budgets, buildings, several kinds of meeting spaces, kitchens, nurseries, lavatories and car parks – all of which are fundamental assets you need for organizing. They also have staff, a cadre of professionally trained leaders, ties to larger denominational structures with greater resources and a widely trusted historical tradition to build upon. Churches are the institution most commonly found in every kind of neighbourhood, across all geographic, racial, cultural and class boundaries. In some poor communities, churches are virtually the last standing institution. In those situations, it's often only the churches that have the moral authority and institutional presence to lead efforts for civic reconstruction. With proximity to the problems, churches can work from the bottom up, redeeming young people one by one, claiming whole blocks and neighbourhoods for transformation, calling for moral, civic and political renewal in the broader community, city and nation.

And, of course, the churches have a constituency. They actually have members – another prerequisite for organizing – who can be mobilized and brought together. The very nature of a universal membership in the faith community can be instrumental in helping to overcome the divisions between people that are the greatest obstacle to organizing. And members of faith communities can be motivated to act not just in their own self-interest, but rather on the basis of the deeply held spiritual and moral values that undergird their faith. That faith can provide the staying power so critically needed for long-term campaigns. Religious institutions also have enduring power, as opposed to some other community institutions that are often here today and gone tomorrow. Most churches plan to be a part of their communities for a very long time, and therefore have a vested interest in their well-being.

Additionally, because churches are built on relationships, they can provide a strong base for the kind of relational organizing style that is proving to be so effective around the country. Community organizer and sociologist Marshall Ganz speaks of this as a 'covenantal' organizing style. He contrasts it with 'issue-based organizing', which is more 'contractual': 'It has a limited, short-term, outcome-based focus; it often brings people into coalitions that dissolve immediately after the objective is attained, or isn't.' Ganz prefers 'interest-based organizing', which is 'covenantal'. It has a longer-term focus of 'identifying and developing those common interests which are affected by a variety of issues that come and go', he says. 'Interest-based organizing places a greater emphasis on building relationships as a way both to discern interests as well as to construct new interests which only emerge in the context of new relationship.'

What Would Jesus Do?

Finally, faith communities also have the enormous advantage of being able to raise the fundamental religious questions that can radically reshape the political conversation. I found myself speaking at Point Loma College, a conservative Christian school in San Diego, California, which, that very night, would be the host city for the 1996 election campaign's second and final presidential debate. The whole town was buzzing about the great event and wondering how one might get into the hall to participate.

I asked the students two simple questions. First, I asked what they would ask Bill Clinton and Bob Dole if they were in the room for the debate. Quickly the hands shot up – the favourite questions were about abortion, lowering taxes ('I'd ask why are my dad's taxes so high') and the president's alleged extramarital affairs. All the first group of questions were more or less what one would expect from the children of affluent suburban Republican and conservative evangelical families in Southern California. Fair questions to be sure, but hardly representing a comprehensive moral agenda. My second question to the students was different. I asked them, 'What would Jesus ask if he were in that hall tonight?'

Now the room was quiet and you could almost feel the students thinking. Very slowly the first hand was raised. 'Jesus would ask them how they were treating the poor.' Then another hand. 'He would probably ask them to treat each other better too.' And a white student said, 'Jesus would certainly have something to say about racism.' These were the same students who just a moment before had acted like anyone else of their race, class and political party. But when the 'Jesus question' was raised, it changed the outcome of the whole discussion.

My mother used to tell us kids that that was always a good question – 'What would Jesus do?' But our own church never asked the question when it came to racism. After years of organizing in the civil rights and anti-war movements, I came back to faith through the same Jesus question. Despite the church's misrepresentations over many years, most people (religious or not) know that Jesus stood for compassion, caring, and justice. Somehow, Jesus has survived the churches and all of us. To invoke the name of Jesus still raises the right questions in relation to social policy, even when religion is not really a part of the conversation. The name of Jesus still has the authority to interrogate our social priorities.

Somehow, the world understands that Jesus stands for 'the least of these' even when the churches don't. That was the great spiritual gap of the twentieth-century church. At the beginning of a new century and millennium, we have to signal something new. And it's already beginning to happen. There is a very popular bracelet worn by millions of young people today that simply displays the letters WWJD, standing for What Would Jesus Do. My

mother was right. And it's a question that could bring many
people together, even far beyond the churches. If you can find a
way to ask such a religious, spiritual or moral question you'll
open a much wider world of possible answers.

Chapter Ten

Be a Contemplative

Do justice, love kindness, and walk humbly
with your God. (Micah 6.8)

I TOOK MY TWO-WEEK-OLD SON to hear Nelson Mandela speak in Harvard Yard. The regal 80-year-old president of South Africa might have been the oldest person in the crowd of 25,000, while Luke Carroll Wallis, comfortably asleep in his pram, might well have been the youngest. Joy and I thought their overlap in history would be a good beginning for our first child. I look forward to telling him about it some day.

Mandela was at Harvard to become only the third person in history to be given an honorary doctorate at a special convocation, the other two being George Washington and Winston Churchill. The world's most respected and honoured political leader told stories, made jokes (about himself mostly), graciously thanked everyone around him, and, characteristically, accepted the honour on behalf of his people. 'We accept this great honour bestowed upon us today', he said. Also characteristically, he called his audience again to go forward in the next step on the road toward justice. 'The greatest single challenge facing our globalized world,' said Nelson Mandela, 'is to combat and eradicate its disparities.' As the planet's most revered practitioner of democracy, Mandela admonished: 'While in all parts of the world, progress is being made in entrenching democratic forms of governance, we constantly need to remind ourselves that the freedoms which democracy brings will remain empty shells if they are not accompanied by real and tangible improvements in the material lives of the millions of ordinary citizens of those countries.'

As a leader, Nelson Mandela is the epitome of discipline and preparation. We must take on an undisciplined society by calling for spiritual *discipline*, which is the key word here. I was a Boy Scout and still remember the motto 'Be Prepared'. It's a good motto for all who would like to change the world or their corner of it. Social movements do require spiritual preparation.

We need the kind of preparation today that enables us to develop a longer-term perspective, find an appropriate spiritual practice, stay focused, learn patience and balance contemplation with action.

Be Prepared

Richard Rohr is both a good friend and a powerful spiritual teacher. Richard is a Franciscan priest who has recently been doing comparative studies of various initiation rites for young men in very diverse cultures, both ancient and contemporary. Initiation rites were characteristically used as an important means of spiritual preparation. Richard believes that our society has virtually lost the practice of initiating young people, especially young men, into mature adulthood, and that the social consequences are painfully evident.

He has found a remarkable similarity in the 'lessons of life' that such rites attempt to teach across both cultures and time. Rohr summarizes these as the following:

1 Life is hard.
2 You're going to die.
3 You're not that important.
4 You're not in control.
5 Life is not just about you.

In a wide variety of cultures, these simple but common themes come through as the critical lessons young people need to assimilate if they ever hope to make the passage to mature adulthood. Now consider how utterly contrary those lessons are to what our modern culture teaches. In fact, one could argue that contemporary society literally turns these spiritual lessons on their head. If we were to compile the list of modern culture's assumptions, they might read:

1   Life can be easy.
2   You can stay young (or keep looking and feeling young) for ever.
3   You are what's most important.
4   Above all else, you must stay in control.
5   Life is mostly about you and your fulfilment.

It's no wonder our young people are confused, not to mention all the rest of us. In a consumer culture that is both highly individualistic and extremely competitive, spiritual formation aimed at the common good isn't too popular. Ironically, however, when people in our society see someone exhibiting spiritual virtues, we are drawn to that person as by a magnet. That phenomenon speaks to our society's great hunger for spiritual meaning and social purpose, despite the opposing messages of popular culture and the marketplace. The ethos of modern advertising may control public discourse but it doesn't satisfy the human soul.

That's why we are so drawn to a Nelson Mandela. He doesn't represent the fast buck, quick fix or immediate gratification. In Harvard Yard, I saw noisy students turn quiet and calm, straining to get just a glimpse of this old man. A faculty member later commented that his 'pushy colleagues' who would normally fight for every square inch on the platform were awed by the magnitude of the man. Somehow he enables others to rise above it all, to transcend the pettiness, to transform the possibilities, to aspire to their better selves. For about two precious hours, Nelson Mandela had the whole Harvard community thinking about someone else and about how they too might help change the world.

I had seen this phenomenon before when I had the blessing to be present in a small meeting with Mandela and US religious leaders shortly after his release from prison, and again at the extraordinary events of his inauguration as the first democratically elected president of South Africa. He has the power to transform people and situations, something we have not seen in a leader for some time.

But why? Is it because he won the Nobel Peace Prize, or the leadership of the African National Congress, or the South African presidency? I don't think so. I believe it is because of what happened to him during 27 years in prison. It was there that Nelson Mandela had his spiritual formation, there that he prepared for a

new nation, there that he began moulding a people – black and
white – to think in new ways.

There are many legends about Nelson Mandela on Robben
Island, his prison home for most of those years. Many have called
Robben Island Mandela University, because every day he was
educating everyone around him to a vision of a new South Africa.
The sweep of his influence was again demonstrated at his
inauguration, when several of his former prison guards were
given honoured seats close to their former prisoner and teacher.
Mandela got up every day to prepare himself, his colleagues and
his captors for a new day. His regimen was physically,
emotionally, intellectually and spiritually vigorous. He had no
guarantee that he would ever live to see the new South Africa, or
that he would ever get out of prison. But he knew that his task
was to get ready. And by all reports, Mandela was utterly
disciplined in that task. Separation from the increasingly shallow
values of the outside Western world might have been a blessing
for this political prisoner.

During Mandela's last visit to America before retiring from the
South African presidency, many people recalled where they were
on 11 February 1990, when Nelson Mandela walked out of prison
in front of the eyes of the world – erect, strong and astonishing.
Some talked of how they woke up their children to witness the
momentous event. He emerged with a spring in his step and a
dignity on his face that belied his years of suffering. Henry Louis
Gates testified in Harvard Yard that he always had a 'Free
Mandela' poster in his college dorm room and later hung it in his
daughter's nursery. Gates said to the Harvard students, 'Nelson
Mandela didn't walk out of prison into freedom, but as one who
had been free the whole time. Mandela has always been free.' In
his sermon the following Sunday, Peter Gomes, the dean of
Harvard's Memorial Chapel, said of Mandela, 'This is a man who
knows who he is. His ideals are intact. He doesn't live with the
illusions of his demons. He does not stagger at the uneven
motions of the world.'

That strength comes from spiritual preparation. There is an
important distinction between power and moral authority that the
modern world fails to understand. Power is the ability to control
things; moral authority is the capacity to change things. Those in
power really don't change anything. They just manage things as
they are, because to gain power they have agreed to accept things

as they are. On the contrary, those with moral authority can transform political realities, in part because they have chosen not to accept the current definitions of those realities. Power depends on coercion; moral authority utilizes inspiration.

Pharaoh had the power, but Moses had the authority. Pilate had the power, but Jesus had the authority. The medieval popes had the power, but Saint Francis had the authority. The British had the power, but Gandhi had the authority. The southern governors had the power, but Martin Luther King, Jr, had the authority. The rulers of apartheid in Pretoria had the power, but Nelson Mandela had the authority. In every case, those with the power are not even remembered now, except in relation to those who had the authority.

But authority doesn't come easily or without cost. It comes only through spiritual preparation and formation. Moses struggled with his calling in the wilderness. Jesus went out into the desert at the onset of his ministry to fast for 40 days. Saint Francis led a life of poverty, chastity and obedience. Martin Luther King, Jr, suffered death threats, 30 arrests and imprisonments, and an assassin's bullet. Nelson Mandela spent 27 years in prison. All had to prepare, all got ready, and all paid the price.

The man who sustained his fellow prisoners now charms all of us. Everyone knows that Nelson Mandela led not by relying on opinion polls but rather by changing people's opinions. He is someone the world believes to have integrity and character. He also was smart enough not to believe his own press cuttings. When you hear Mandela speak, genuine humility and humanity come through, traits we are unfamiliar with in most political leaders today. Mandela knows who he is. And that is not a perfect person, nor one without sin and flaws, nor someone who hasn't made mistakes.

It was amazing to see every political leader – even former segregationists like Senator Strom Thurmond – in Washington clamouring to get near to Mandela when he came to receive the Congressional Gold Medal on 23 September 1998. Integrity brings people together and crosses partisan political lines. And here is where leaders with moral authority always differ from their counterparts with political power only: they are not interested in revenge. As Harvard's Neil Rudenstine said, 'He never sought to harm those who harmed him, or to punish his abusers. He looks forward to justice, not backward to revenge.'

Mandela smiled at the crowd often during his speech at Harvard, and accused the students of coming just to 'see how a man of 80 looks'. Then he looked seriously at the crowd and said, 'There is no easy walk to freedom, but it is the only walk worth taking.' Mandela inspires me like no other modern political leader. But it is time for him to rest now. He spoke of that in his speech at the United Nations on 21 September 1998.

> I have reached that part of the long walk when the opportunity is granted, as it should be to all men and women, to retire to some rest and tranquillity in the village of my birth. As I sit in Qunu and grow as ancient as its hills, I will continue to entertain the hope that there has emerged a cadre of leaders in my own country and region, on my continent and in the world, which will not allow that any should be denied their freedom as we were; that any should be turned into refugees as we were; that any should be condemned to go hungry as we were; that any should be stripped of their human dignity as we were.
>
> Were all these hopes to translate into a realizable dream and not a nightmare to torment the soul of the aged, then will I, indeed, have peace and tranquillity.

Are we preparing the way for those kinds of leaders?

The Nature of Leadership

For more than a year, President Clinton argued that he should be judged on the basis of his policies, and that personal moral failures, while regrettable, were not really relevant to the job he was doing for the American people.

I often felt politically homeless during the Clinton scandal. Most Democrats and liberals ended up making excuses for Clinton and defending him. I wasn't comfortable with that. But the Republicans ended up looking like the Pharisees who were ready to stone the woman taken in adultery. And while I often agreed with the conservatives on how much Clinton was morally damaging the country, I was uncomfortable with their broader political agenda.

An old friend and I decided to write about the problem. He is a denominational church leader – Wes Granberg-Michaelson leads the Reformed Church in America – and was formerly chief of staff to US Senator Mark Hatfield. We tried to reflect upon the lessons the country learned or failed to learn in the course of the nation's year-long Washington-produced drama of sex and politics. And we asked what lasting wisdom about leadership would be left after the curtain was drawn and this morality play went off the air.

In an editorial commentary piece for the *Chicago Tribune*, Wes and I suggested that this sad chapter in American history could turn out to be a teachable moment on the nature of leadership, and that the country shouldn't miss this opportunity to reflect upon it. These are not Left or Right issues, and they have little to do with whether or not one supported Bill Clinton's political agenda.

First, effective public leadership cannot be severed from the trustworthiness of personal character. Ethics and integrity do matter, and not just superficially. Leaders need to be believed. They have to engender trust not only in their policies but also in their judgement. They must create a climate of faithfulness to shared commitments among colleagues and supporters. Thus leadership derives credibility from example, and not simply from pronouncements. In times of crisis, people follow courage rather than charm.

The final years of the Clinton presidency illustrate a successful leadership that skilfully segregated public policy from personal integrity. Morality in politics, especially for many Democrats, is defined only by the pragmatic effectiveness of policies. Conversely, many Republicans see morality exclusively in terms of personal behaviour and are blind to the sins of social injustice. This will not work. And religious people should be the first to say so. A firewall between the personal and public dimensions of our lives is a secular fiction. And it is dangerous to both people and politics. Faith nurtures a healthy congruity between one's inner and outer lives. Its understanding of sin and its vision of wholeness weave together the social and the personal. Any discerning ethic of leadership does the same.

Second, a poll-driven presidency lacks a moral foundation and vision. Faced with perhaps the most important personal decision of his presidency, Clinton trusted his pollsters rather than his pastors. Some leaders have the moral and political authority to shape, and even change, public opinion. But for that, a moral compass is needed – a compass whose needle points toward where we, as a society, should be heading, rather than simply

toward the next election. Politicians today try to govern by
perpetual campaigns. As a result, the overriding principle is to
satisfy 51 per cent of the voters rather than to serve a compelling
moral and political vision for our society.

Third, style is not more important than substance. Democrats,
liberals and progressives kept saying that Clinton was a good
president even if he could be a better man. But Clinton was more
style than substance. If a Republican president had done many of
the things that Bill Clinton did in his domestic and foreign
policies, there would have been a Democratic outcry, but with a
Democrat in charge, hardly a peep was heard. Clinton maintained
a liberal language and cultural style, and for most liberals that
seemed to be enough. But is being comfortable in black churches
and even appointing a record number of minorities and women
to government posts enough to counterbalance cosying up to
Wall Street and playing to suburban voters while virtually
abandoning the underclass? The attacks upon him by right-wing
conservatives somehow made liberals even more defensive of
Clinton.

Fourth, sexual ethics are important. You don't have to be a
prude or a puritan to be worried about a sexual ethic that is
merely recreational instead of covenantal. That value-free sexual
ethic has devastating consequences for a society, especially for
the young, and most brutally for the poor. Clinton didn't create
the nation's declining sexual ethics, but the Clinton scandal served
to reveal them and help support them.

The question 'What's more important, a leader's personal
morality or his or her public policy?' may really be the wrong one.
The more important issue may be the *connection* between the
personal and the public. The idea that public leadership can be
partitioned from personal integrity is, as most of us should know,
a dangerous illusion. And the fact that several past political
leaders have got away with doing so hardly establishes a reliable
pattern of leadership for the future. Old styles of leadership are
now passing, and new models are already in formation.

The information revolution has subverted the systems of
hierarchical authority, transforming our institutions and the
imperatives of leadership. The task of leaders today is to articulate
vision, build trust and create an open climate of integrity that
facilitates decisions. Any leader who wants to be a leader in the
twenty-first century needs to sustain values, nurture community

and clarify common mission. That is equally true for a pastor, a principal, a president or a pope.

In the end, leaders lead by behaviour and not just by skill. And in any institution, people yearn for leadership that is morally seamless. Yes, they want imaginative and effective policies. But they also desire leaders whose example walks their talk. A healthier blend of talent and character is needed to shape our next generation of leaders.

That coherence is quite different from the futile quest for leaders whom we hope are perfect. Those of us who seek to embed our lives in religious faith know full well the tenacity of selfish, sinful behaviour. The power, adulation and pressure inherent in positions of leadership make leaders more likely to fall victim to their own vulnerabilities – whether it is pride, promiscuity or political prostitution. But because of this reality, leaders in particular need to undertake the difficult task of self-examination. That's why leaders bear a particular responsibility to nurture their private souls and not just their public personas.

We all have flaws, as Jesus was quick to point out to those who would have stoned the adulterous woman. But we don't get past our flaws by denying them and trying to manage the public fallout. In his or her heart, every leader knows that this denial – in the words of Jesus – is the path to destruction.

Mature leaders are those who not only rely on their strengths but also learn how to deal consciously with their weaknesses. In some safe and secure place, they bring their brokenness into the light and turn toward inner coherence. Thus they guard themselves against the disintegration of their inward life that could finally result in outward paralysis. Dealing with flaws and weaknesses is important for anyone, but especially for those who have responsibility for others.

In the future, we need leaders with the ability to navigate the troubled waters of their inner lives as well as the turbulent seas of public discourse. If institutions and societies are ultimately shaped by both the personal and the public ethics of their leaders, the concept of 'spiritual formation' should become increasingly important as a component of the education needed for leadership development. Ultimately, personal integrity is vital to public trust.

Leadership instils vision, values, trust, mission and community. These rest upon the habits of the heart. Perhaps the main question to ask about leaders concerns the trustworthiness of their moral compass, upon which all of their judgments depend. Effective leadership is finally sustained not just by what people say but by who they are.

The Contemplative Life

Henri Nouwen was the author of dozens of books on spirituality. A native of the Netherlands who lived and worked in North America, he was a friend and a frequent visitor to Sojourners. When he died in 1996, eulogies praised him as one of the most significant spiritual writers of the century. Nouwen understood that spirituality had social implications, and his writings are rich material for reflection.

To make that connection between the spiritual and the social wasn't always easy for a contemplative like Henri. We spent many hours talking together about his struggle to make justice and peace an essential part of his walk with Jesus. From Selma to Atlanta, from Nicaragua to Peru, from the Nevada nuclear test site to the Peace Pentecost demonstrations in Washington, DC, he tried to connect the inner life with the outward journey. Henri was never at home with big marches and crowds or with the intensity of political activism. Yet he would often call to ask whether he could be part of an event or action, such as an all-night prayer vigil in the midst of great controversy over an issue like the Gulf War. He knew he had to stretch himself by taking his prayers to the streets because, in spite of his private personality, his spirituality sought to connect with those active efforts for justice and peace.

I have often wished that many activists would similarly stretch themselves by linking their actions to contemplation. The essential element of the quest for justice and peace for Nouwen was prayer. But finding time for prayer, and even for some quiet contemplation, is a constant challenge for an activist.

Henri also spoke about the 'three disciplines' of the contemplative life. All three are essential to the life of an activist. Yet 'disciplines' is indeed the right word, because the contemplative life does not come easily to any of us. Nouwen's disciplines of solitude, community and ministry would deepen the life and work of anyone who wants to change a community.

The first discipline is the discipline of solitude. It's only in solitude that we can get in touch with the Spirit of God in us.

Solitude is an important discipline in a busy world. Solitude involves prayer, spiritual reading, and being alone with God.

The second discipline is the discipline of community. Out of solitude we go into community. Community is not just a place where we do things together, but a place where together we recognize the presence of God...Community, whether a parish, a family, or an intentional community, is where people live together and want to discover in each other the presence of God.

The third discipline is ministry, reaching out to others. It's important to reach out to others because we want to share from the abundance of our life, not because we have a need to be good helpers or because we have something to prove.

Nouwen knew the importance of a spiritual life of faith deeply rooted in an intimate communion with God. But he also knew the importance of an active commitment to healing the brokenness of the world. For example, Henri wrote on the question of Christ's judgement, 'As long as there are strangers; hungry, naked, and sick people; prisoners, refugees, and slaves; people who are handicapped physically, mentally, or emotionally; people without work, a home, or a piece of land, there will be that haunting question from the throne of judgment: "What have you done for the least of mine?"'

I remember one weekend Henri visited Sojourners. That particular weekend, Brazilian archbishop Dom Helder Câmara was also in town to speak to a large church convention in a downtown hotel. We got a call from Dom Helder's aides saying that he felt uncomfortable in the big, fancy hotel and wanted to spend the afternoon in a base community like Sojourners. We were thrilled, and I hurried across the invisible racial and class boundaries of DC to pick up the diminutive and passionate prelate of the people from Recife, Brazil.

The community quickly gathered, and the next few hours we spent together were memorable ones – highlighted by the dialogue between Henri Nouwen and Dom Helder Câmara. The Dutch priest from the first world was one of the most intense people I have ever met, and his questions to the archbishop from the third world were relentless. That afternoon, Henri seemed to sense that there were truths he would never find in the affluent first world, that it was among the despised and rejected of the third world that his search would have to continue. Later, he

would leave the academic cocoons of Yale and Harvard to make
his own pilgrimage into Latin America, and he wouldn't really find
a home until he entered into sharing a life with the mentally and
physically handicapped of L'Arche Daybreak Community near
Toronto, in Canada.

The intensity of his spiritual search is what I will always most
remember about Henri. He could spend hours with you – talking,
walking, and very often anguishing about the deepest questions of
life and faith. He was not a Christian who had it all figured out. On
the contrary, Henri wrestled like Jacob with the God he so dearly
loved. And that made him wrestle with all of us, too.

The shock of his sudden death from a heart attack on an
aeroplane lingered for some time. But his legacy continues with
those whose faith drives them both to retreat centres and to the
streets. Plucked from us before his time, like another monastic
named Thomas Merton, Henri Nouwen leaves us a rich legacy
and a whole library of spiritual struggle. Through his endless
stream of books, the countless students he touched, L'Arche
residents who touched him, and the thousands and thousands of
people who attended the regular and intimate Eucharists he
insisted upon having wherever he was, Henri's spiritual intensity
will live on. I can only give thanks for Henri Nouwen's life and
witness, and be grateful that Henri is finally at rest in the arms of
the loving God who always pursued him like the hound of
heaven.

The Hope of Results

To be a contemplative means to find a motivation deeper than the
hope of results. You have to be sustained by more important
things. And anyone who gets involved in the struggle for social
change may eventually confront the problem of burnout. It was
that other monastic, the Trappist monk Thomas Merton, who
spoke so eloquently to this problem, common especially among
social activists. He did so in 'A Letter to a Young Activist', sent to a
young man named Jim Forest. Jim is older now, yet still very much
involved as a peace activist in the Netherlands. I recall many late-
night conversations with Jim, talking about the problem of
burnout. We spoke of the faith that sometimes can help people
persevere in the face of seemingly hopeless struggles. And how
that faith must ultimately depend not on the hope of results,

especially in the short term, but on something deeper. It is a paradox: to be successful you must finally give up the demand for success and do what you do from the deeper motivations of what you believe is right. And this isn't a merely religious issue; I've known non-religious people who stick to their principles and causes long after many church types have given up and gone home. Ultimately, you must find a reason to continue that derives its satisfactions from the truth of the work itself. Then, when results do come, they can be welcomed as a surprising grace rather than as the necessary vindication for exhausting and despairing work.

We end here with the letter that Thomas Merton sent to Forest in 1966, during a period when he felt 'pretty close to burn-out'. Merton died in 1968, but this letter has been reprinted many times and in various languages over the past 30 years. It's a good thing to put up on your wall. It will help you to understand how to be a contemplative.

Dear Jim,

Do not depend on the hope of results. When you are doing the sort of work you have taken on, essentially an apostolic work, you may have to face the fact that your work will be apparently worthless and even achieve no result at all, if not perhaps results opposite to what you expect. As you get used to this idea, you start more and more to concentrate not on the results but on the value, the rightness, the truth of the work itself. And there too a great deal has to be gone through, as gradually you struggle less and less for an idea and more and more for specific people. The range tends to narrow down, but it gets much more real. In the end, it is the reality of personal relationships that saves everything.

You are fed up with words, and I don't blame you. I am nauseated by them sometimes. I am also, to tell the truth, nauseated by ideals and with causes. This sounds like heresy, but I think you will understand what I mean. It is so easy to get engrossed with ideas and slogans and myths that in the end one is left holding the bag, empty, with no trace of meaning left in it. And then the temptation is to yell louder than ever in order to make the meaning be there again by magic. Going through this kind of reaction helps you to guard against this. Your system is complaining of too much verbalizing, and it is right.

The big results are not in your hands or mine, but they suddenly happen and we can share in them; but there is no point in building our lives on this personal satisfaction, which may be denied us and which after all is not that important.

The next step in the process is for you to see that your own thinking about what you are doing is crucially important. You are probably striving to build yourself an identity in your work, out of your work and your witness. You are using it, so to speak, to protect yourself against nothingness, annihilation. That is not the right use of your work. All the good that you will do will come not from you but from the fact that you have allowed yourself, in the obedience of faith, to be used by God's love. Think of this more, and gradually you will be free from the need to prove yourself, and you can be more open to the power that will work through you without your knowing it.

The great thing after all is to live, not to pour out your life in the service of a myth: and we turn the best things into myths. If you can get free from the domination of causes and just serve Christ's truth, you will be able to do more and will be less crushed by the inevitable disappointments. Because I see nothing whatever in sight but much disappointment, frustration and confusion...

The real hope, then, is not in something we think we can do but in God who is making something good out of it in some way we cannot see. If we can do His will, we will be helping in this process. But we will not necessarily know all about it beforehand...

Enough of this... it is at least a gesture... I will keep you in my prayers.

All the best, in Christ,

Tom

Chapter Eleven

Keep it Human

For we have this treasure in earthen vessels.
(2 Corinthians 4.7)

LET ME EXPLAIN what I mean by keeping it human. In the struggle for social change, it is very important to take care of one another – our families, our kids and ourselves. The human dimension is so easy to lose and so crucial to maintain. It's so important to stay grounded, not get too grandiose or self-important, keep humble and, above all, keep your sense of humour. Heavy tasks and important work often require a certain lightheartedness. And that arises from a place of freedom rather than compulsion, from giving up the illusions of control and trusting results to God. We have to learn how to enjoy the world while we try to change it. After all, changing our communities should not only be challenging; it should also be fun.

Social change is not easy; it's often very frustrating. And there are as many lessons in the setbacks, difficulties and even failures, as there are in the successes. It's important to be as honest about the problems and the defeats as it is about the victories.

The hardest things are not always what you would expect. I've found that living in the inner city, travelling to dangerous war zones and going to jail have not been the hardest things. Though they have often been the most exciting. Most difficult for me have been the personal failures and the breakdown of relationships.

While community creates a powerful resource for change, it also generates real tensions among people. I've learned those lessons firsthand, when our own Sojourners Community experienced a painful split in the early 1990s. We had always talked about growing up and old together, and we believed our relationships could sustain many challenges. But some of the young families didn't want to bring up their children in the inner city (which was a reasonable concern), and those who stayed felt disappointed and even betrayed by those who left (which was also understandable). Differences in vision arose too, and personality conflicts ensued (or was it the other way around?). And the inevitable conflicts over leadership emerged. I had seen the same tensions in many other small communities and projects and had often been called in to be a mediator. Now it was happening in my own community, and I felt helpless to do anything about it.

I learned then that we can invest too much in community as well as too little. Our expectations can be too high and quite unrealistic. In a society of rampant individualism, there is a danger of over-reacting and defining community in ways that are both too intense and too close. People need space, even in community, and that's especially true for families.

The breakups that occur closest to home are the ones that hurt the most. Sometimes the intensity of the vision and the pace of the work can wreak havoc in the marriages and families of activists. The rate of divorce, which is so tragically high in our contemporary society, is sometimes even higher among those who are trying to change the world. My own short-lived first marriage was one of those casualties. The pain and self-doubt that came from that personal failure were more difficult than all the disappointments and set-backs of years of social action.

An important lesson learned from communal and personal breakups is the crucial value of our relationships, especially with our spouses and children. The very best causes and visions can turn us into people far too driven by the desire for success and results. The temptations to overwork, the dangers of pride and self-importance and the severe burdens of the cause can drive the joy from our lives. It is vital to maintain a balance between the cause and our own lives, and, in fact, I've noticed that both family and friendships seem to become increasingly important over the long haul. The good news is that our mistakes don't need to ruin our lives. Grace, new beginnings and second chances are always possible, as I've discovered in my own life.

Always remember that when you're dealing with projects and

campaigns, you're dealing with people. Just as the work for justice can inspire and call forth our best selves, our worst selves can also become very evident in the process. Competition, ego, pride, money, sex and power have often foiled the most hopeful efforts for change. Some of the greatest tragedies I've ever witnessed have been the personal falls from influence and power of some social-movement leaders who had the greatest potential. I've been close enough to several of those tragedies to observe both the rise and the fall, and to see how it all happens. It teaches you the critical importance of personal integrity in the struggle for social change. Shortcuts in personal ethics will usually have long-term consequences.

Financial or sexual corruption is often involved in the great public falls, but the deeper moral issue is usually the corruption of power. Our society needs more leadership and less celebrity, more character and less charisma. Clear mechanisms for the accountability of leadership have proved to be key for the integrity of social movements and causes. The old adage 'Practise what you preach' is still the best guide.

Don't Forget to Have Fun

At the end of Dorothy Day's life, everybody wanted to meet and talk with her. The steady flow of visitors to New York City's Mary House often tired her out. Some of the young volunteers working there at the Catholic Worker were most insistent. One day, several of them approached her, hoping to persuade her to join them in a big demonstration against nuclear weapons at the United Nations. Mass arrests were expected at the planned UN sit-in, and she guessed that the youthful activists were secretly wanting to tell their children one day that they had once been arrested with Dorothy Day. Dorothy, however, was quite unenthusiastic. 'I've done that enough times already; you go ahead without me,' she told them. 'Oh, please, Dorothy,' they replied. 'It would be such a great experience!' After their repeated efforts to change her mind, Dorothy finally said, 'Look, if I came along, here's what would happen. We would all be sitting in a circle, and the police would come. They would take all of you away and leave me for last because I'm so old. I'd be sitting there alone. Finally, the police would all be standing over me, shaking their heads, and asking, "What are you doing here?" And I'd probably forget!'

Along with humour, music is essential to any successful movement for social change. If a movement doesn't produce good jokes and good songs, it probably isn't worth joining. Emma Goldman is renowned for her famous quip 'If I can't dance, I won't join your revolution'. Where would we be without Woody Guthrie, Pete Seeger and all the minstrels of the civil rights movement? Singing together is probably one of the most bonding experiences people have. And those who were in the inner circle of the civil rights movement report the raucous atmosphere of jokes and pranks that kept Martin Luther King, Jr, and his closest associates sane during the most difficult, frightening and violent of times.

Common Grace

Sometimes people working for change can become far too ideological, or even far too spiritual, about things. They just need to lighten up a little and find the grace abundant in this world, especially in the most common of experiences. I've mentioned some of my own encounters with such grace, often in the form of second chances. That's what happened for me when I met Joy Carroll, an Anglican priest from south London. We met on a panel discussion in front of 2,000 young people attending the Greenbelt arts festival. Because of the breakup of my earlier marriage, I had given up on the kind of personal happiness that isn't dependent on the results of work or the successes of campaigns. Joy made me believe in it again.

After a two-year transatlantic romance, Joy Carroll and I were married on 25 October 1997, in Immanuel Church, Streatham, south London, where she had been serving as a priest. A wonderful service and lively reception complete with Indian food (our favourite) was followed by a great English community party, where we danced the night away. Highlights for my siblings, who had flown across the Atlantic for the big event, were my father being pulled on to the dance floor by an exuberant woman from Joy's church and, by the end of the evening, the sight of my parents dancing cheek to cheek. Cameras were quickly out to record the first time any of us ever saw my parents dance, as far as we could remember. Even for them, the occasion seemed to call for dancing.

Joy is the kind of person who's learned that having a great time is part of the Christian life. She'll often ask me, 'What are we going to do for fun today?' I confess that I hadn't asked that question often before. Having been one of the first women ordained in the Church of England, who took a parish in one of London's toughest housing estates, served as the youngest member of the church's governing synod, and was called upon to be a frequent public and media spokesperson for women and other marginalized people, Joy knows the struggle for justice. But she also knows when to take a break or have a party.

One of the most fun things Joy did was to serve as the script consultant and role model for the highly successful British comedy series *The Vicar of Dibley*, a very humorous look at the trials and tribulations of a female country priest, starring the famous comedy actress Dawn French. South London is a long way from the fictitious Dibley, and the television magazines made quite a story about 'the real vicar of Dibley'. The BBC followed with a television profile of Joy and her inner-city work entitled 'Not the Vicar of Dibley'. When we got married, Dawn and her husband, British comedian Lenny Henry, came to the wedding, which was dutifully covered by the British tabloids (THE REAL VICAR OF DIBLEY MARRIES!). That made for an interesting first day of our honeymoon beach holiday as we peered through our sunglasses at tourists reading the story of our wedding in the *Daily Mail*. The irony of it all had two seriously dedicated urban activists chuckling all day.

The surprise of meeting Joy Carroll, developing a fresh relationship in the midst of many responsibilities, and then settling into a new married life has taught me lessons I'd never really known before. They are about the grace of God, who gives second chances, the satisfactions that go deeper than the best of good work, and the personal happiness that changes one's perception of the most mundane realities of everyday life. As I said in my groom's speech, 'I've found a wonderful woman of great substance and deep passion, and these days feel like the best days of my life.' I'm learning that keeping substance and passion together is the key.

At 6.56 p.m., 3 September 1998, Luke Carroll Wallis came into the world. Seven pounds, seven ounces, and 20 inches long were the vital statistics. More vital was a healthy baby who entered the world without distress in a good natural labour. Sporting lots of dark hair and big blue eyes, Luke went straight to his mother's breast and to his happy parents' hearts. For both of us, he is a first child. And the first week of Luke's life was full of pure delights.

Helping him learn to feed, watching him sleep, giving him his first
bath, getting to know every part of his little body, interacting with
those lovely blue eyes, taking him out for his first walk and
enjoying people's smiles and attention, wondering about his
future, smiling at each other a lot – those were the initial wonders
for Joy and me. Our world was full of light.

I often reflected, throughout that first week, how universal these
experiences are. Parents rich and poor, of all colours, and in every
culture and nation have known these delights for millennia. Having
a baby is the most common thing in the world. And yet each little
part of welcoming this new life into your life seems unique and
special to the parents and family involved. That's common grace. It
is indeed a gift from God, and nothing makes us more aware of how
precious God's gifts are than a newborn baby. Life itself seems more
precious to us than it ever did before. Again, an almost universal
experience for parents.

Perhaps that's why our hearts go out to them when we see other
little babies threatened by famine, war or extreme poverty. This is
not supposed to happen to them. Everything in you wants to
protect and nurture your child. I now can imagine what the parents
of those greatly-at-risk children must feel when they are unable to
protect them. As new parents, we didn't really know that in
addition to loving each other, we could love someone else so much
and so immediately. It's a powerful feeling and one, we suspect,
that God has a great deal to do with.

Holding Luke in the delivery room, I did pray, as many parents
do, that he would be everything that God desires of him and
created him to be. Offering your child to God is a way of offering
yourself to God again, and it felt that way to me. For the religious
and for those who are not, there is powerful spirituality in the birth
of a child. Already we're learning a little about the unconditional
love of God for us through the way we feel about our own child.
Through one of the most universal human experiences, parent
after parent is taught the lessons of love and life. And all this is
grace.

Bound Together

My dear friend Yvonne Delk has a wonderful phrase, 'binding
covenant relationships'. As an African-American woman and
powerful preacher, she speaks movingly about those relationships

that bind people together in covenants of friendship across all humanly conceived barriers and divisions. The phrase means sticking together no matter what, and going through together whatever comes along. Having people like that in your life is perhaps the best way to keep everything very human.

I'll never forget a very dramatic moment in the Rotunda of the US Capitol, when 55 religious leaders stood reading Scripture, praying and singing in response to the nation's changing welfare policy. 'Woe to you legislators!' echoed the voices quoting Isaiah, Chapter 10. Standing in a circle, wearing full clerical garb, the clergy made a strong visual statement.

A group of eighth graders from a Virginia Catholic school happened to be in the Rotunda when the clergy arrived. They were there for a civics lesson and were getting an earful about the practice of democracy. The young people became very quiet, and ventured close to the clergy circle. At that moment, the Capitol police announced through a loudspeaker that the ministers would be arrested if they didn't stop praying. They all stood their ground, and the authorities began to handcuff and lead the clerics away, one at a time. The students watched in silence, but when the last pastor had been taken away, they burst into applause for the ministers.

Both the *New York Times* and National Public Radio were on hand, and immediately approached the young students to get their response. 'What did you learn today?' asked the reporters. 'Unity,' said one young man. 'That you should all come together if you want to fight something; you can't do it independently.' Then a young woman said, 'Today taught me about courage. Sometimes you just have to stand up for something.' Another student agreed. 'But when you do stand up,' he said, 'it's really good to have some other people with you!'

Courage can come from those binding covenant relationships that Yvonne talks about. It was evident that day in the jail cell. For more than 12 hours, before we were finally released with a court date, the religious leaders deepened their relationships. I sat for a while between Christian evangelist Tony Campolo and Jewish rabbi Michael Lerner as they discussed points of convergence and differences in their respective faiths. I watched black clergy talk about the experience of jail during the civil rights movement with white pastors who were experiencing it for the first time. There were no phones, no appointments and no projects to finish. We just hung out in the jail cell together and got close. I've learned it is those kinds of relationships that will keep us human and carry us through whatever we have to face.

A Cloud of Witnesses

In my study, above the desk where I write, is a wall full of pictures. I've put up photos of many of the people who have inspired or nurtured me over the years. Most I never met, but a few I've had the privilege to know. Many of them are referred to in this book. There are Martin Luther King, Jr and Malcolm X, who led the movement that shaped my view of the world. Mentors like William Stringfellow, Daniel Berrigan and Dorothy Day are prominently featured. South African leaders Nelson Mandela, Desmond Tutu and Steve Biko are all here, along with Beyers Naudé, the white church leader who was defrocked as a minister for opposing apartheid. There are people like Clarence Jordan, a white peanut farmer and Bible scholar who stuck his neck out to establish an interracial community and farm in rural Georgia in the 1950s. Some, like Gandhi, caused great changes to occur in the world, while others, like the monk Thomas Merton, caused people to think in entirely different ways. Some, such as archbishops Oscar Romero and Dom Helder Câmara, were established and comfortable church leaders until they spoke out for justice and found themselves under attack or even were killed. They include both the famous and the obscure: the renowned German pastor Dietrich Bonhoeffer, who stood up to Hitler and was hanged, and the little-known Austrian peasant Franz Jagerstatter, who refused to serve in the Third Reich's army and was summarily executed. There are powerful women like Sojourner Truth and Harriet Tubman, who challenged several kinds of injustice at the same time. Some were very learned, like theologian Karl Barth, and some had little formal education, like Mississippi sharecropper and civil rights leader Fannie Lou Hamer, who challenged the Democratic party to be more democratic. Some, like activist Jean Sindab and journalist Penny Lernoux, are dear departed friends or co-workers who, while not famous, made a difference to the lives of many people.

The first time I read books by or about my heroes, I was hungry to learn about their ideas and their accomplishments. What I learned inspired and guided me. But now what I look for in the books and stories about their lives are the more human things. What were their weaknesses, as well as their strengths? How did they connect their personal lives with their public personae? In particular, how did they cope with failure, as well as success? I want to learn how they lived their lives, including their personal and family lives, not just how they shared their ideas or accomplished their work. I want to learn about their humanity. From my heroes, I want to learn two things now: not only what to live for but also how to live.

In the process of that learning, I've discovered how utterly human they all were – and are – even in the midst of their greatness. And that is the greatest comfort of all. Because if we are going to change the world, we've got to keep it human.

Chapter Twelve

Have a Dream

They shall all sit under their own vines and under their own fig trees, and no one shall make them afraid. (Micah 4.4)

MARTIN LUTHER KING, JR, gave his most famous speech at the Lincoln Memorial on 28 August 1963. 'I have a dream' became his most frequently quoted line. His dream had to do with both a vision and an agenda. King called his vision the beloved community. And his agenda concerned civil rights, voting rights and, later, economic justice and peace. The vision of the beloved community was the foundation for the agenda of the civil rights movement. It was and is both powerful and compelling. But visions don't mean much if they are not tied to concrete agendas and campaigns to advance them. Without the practical agendas of civil rights and voting rights, King would have remained only a visionary dreamer, not 'a drum major for justice', the epitaph he chose for himself. Visions have to be expressed in practical agendas.

Throughout this book, we've used the biblical vision of justice, exemplified by both the Hebrew prophets and Jesus, that upholds the dignity of every person as a child of God. But how will that vision become practical? I love the vision of the biblical prophet Micah quoted above. It's a picture of justice and security – everyone beneath their own vine and fig tree, living in peace and unafraid; everybody having enough of economic life to sustain them, without being threatened by anybody else. It's a wonderful vision.

Are there priorities and campaigns that exemplify the vision today? I believe there are – some critical commitments that begin to implement that vision in the real world, or at least bring us closer to it. Taken together they form a real agenda for justice in our day.

Priorities

Children

I believe we could create a broad consensus about our collective responsibility to children, especially those most at risk. The facts alone are stark. In the wealthiest nation in the history of the world, 17 per cent of all our children live in poverty. That jumps to 30 per cent of all Hispanic children and 33 per cent of black children. (In contrast, in Sweden and Belgium 2 per cent of children live in poverty; in Germany, 6 per cent; and in Britain, 9 per cent.) These children did not choose the adverse circumstances that their society, economy and many of their families have thrust upon them. 'Putting children first' is becoming a rallying cry from many quarters. Most people really do care about kids. A serious discussion of a real safety net for children, as well as the opportunities each child deserves as a right of citizenship, could become a first order of public business if we commit to make it so, and that conversation could certainly transcend our political divisions. The religious community especially is moving in this direction because the first priority of a 'biblical politics' is how the poor and vulnerable are treated, and the children we have simply left behind are a litmus test for any notion of a moral politics. Just as we succeeded in ending poverty for most of our older citizens through deliberate social policies, we could do the same for our youngest. Try this: Whenever a debate is going on in your community about a contentious social or political issue, just raise the question of what the impact of the decision will be on the kids. That won't provide easy answers but tends to focus the questions in the right way.

Diversity

The goal here is to view America's growing racial diversity more as a gift to be embraced than as a problem to be solved. That's a fundamental attitude that all of us can commit ourselves to. The old notions of a melting pot must give way to a healthy cultural pluralism supported by an underlying national unity. Racial justice and reconciliation must be taught to our children as non-negotiable principles, and the best way to do that is for adults to act on those principles. Children learn what they see. We must also speak publicly about the root problem of white privilege, and show how it distorts and diminishes life for everybody – including white people. Overcoming our racial divisions is crucial as we begin the new century. Whether we are brought together or further divided must become a moral criterion for evaluating our political goals and processes. Despite evidences of growing racial polarization, we are also witnessing a deep desire for racial reconciliation in many quarters, including some unexpected places. The leadership being offered by a new generation of black and Hispanic urban leaders is winning respect across the political spectrum. If the young leaders of America's diverse minorities can forge a common interest in breaking down the walls of white privilege instead of fighting with one another, they will accomplish significant social victories, especially if they can form effective alliances with young whites who find the old racial privilege more a burden than a blessing.

Family

Family is becoming an issue that crosses political boundaries, as parents of all political stripes face a culture increasingly hostile to bringing up children.

There is an opportunity here. Protecting and sustaining the bonds that nurture us as we raise our young could become a central priority for both cultural affirmation and public policy, and many across the political spectrum would support that. And we can learn that seeking to nurture a critical mass of healthy, self-sustaining two-parent families does not preclude protecting the rights of those who don't fit the traditional pattern; in fact, justice requires it. Let's talk about the importance of family values every chance we can, not as a code language for pitched battles between Left and Right, but rather as a commitment we all make to the kind of loving and caring families capable of bringing up our children and holding our society together.

Community

Reweaving the bonds of both family and community is essential to our collective well-being. I know we're all busy, but even busy people find the time to do the things that are their highest priorities. We all need to help re-create communal institutions and spaces for connecting, which are the antidote for the loneliness, spiritual malnutrition and dangerous isolation that can result in the terrible tragedies we have seen in our schools. Families must connect to neighbourhoods, which connect to communities, which connect to nations.

Ethics

Ideological confrontation has exhausted itself in polarized extremes that fail to resolve deep moral debates. At the same time, there is a new conversation about ethics and public life going on almost anywhere you turn these days. Perhaps more serious discussion of ethics may help us to transcend some of the ideological conflicts that have led to so many political dead ends. We have to learn to talk about issues in new ways. I believe that many people want to move beyond the old entrenched battle lines and talk about the spiritual values that should undergird our social and political life. Searching for some common ground must become more important than merely organizing against our opponents. All of us can do that, wherever we are. We will find it very challenging, but it is absolutely necessary if we are ever to resolve our endless conflicts around incendiary issues such as abortion, family values and gay rights. Learning to talk more carefully about volatile issues is critically important. I believe we are beginning to see the outlines of such a common-ground politics.

Sweatshop Initiatives

One average-size church in Brooklyn, New York, began a campaign that led the Gap clothing company to end its sweatshop activity in El Salvador. Momentum for this movement began when Christian parents looked at labels on the clothes their children were wearing and realized that they were participating in the exploitation of children's labour in other parts of the world. People of Faith Network came into being in 1994, as the Lafayette Avenue Presbyterian Church in Brooklyn became aware of the growing economic injustices of the wage gap, stagnant worker wages and the epidemic growth of sweatshops. Under the leadership of the Revd David Dyson, the congregation drew on their New York connections to create a national network of clergy and lay people who would mobilize campaigns for political and economic justice. As a result of their efforts, People of Faith was instrumental in obtaining a strict code of conduct for Gap, including the rehiring of workers fired because of union activity and the formation of an independent team of human rights monitors in the plants.

The US General Accounting Office's working definition of a 'sweatshop' is 'an employer that violates more than one federal or state labour, industrial homework, occupational safety and health, workers' compensation, or industry registration law'. What this definition means in reality is exploitative wages, harsh and unsafe working conditions, long hours, arbitrary discipline and even harassment.

While not all garment workers are employed by sweatshops, the Department of Labor estimates that more than half of the United States' 22,000 sewing shops violate minimum-wage and overtime laws. Furthermore, over 75 per cent violate safety and health laws, posing a 'substantial probability of death or serious physical harm', according to the department. Also, most workers are immigrants, particularly women, who fear being fired or even deported if they challenge the illegal conditions or abuse. 'When we told the truth about our subminimum wages to a monitor, we were fired,' said Samuel Guerra, a garment worker for 15 years in Los Angeles, who reported to the advocacy group Sweatshop Watch. Guerra's wife and daughter, who worked in the same factory, were fired as well.

Furthermore, the garment industry extends beyond the borders of the US into areas where labour is viewed as even cheaper. For example, Sweatshop Watch documents that workers in Vietnam average 12 cents an hour, while those in Honduras make about 60 cents. Co-op America reports on the gap between sweatshop wages and corporate profits: 'At the Chentex Factory in the Free Trade Zone in Nicaragua, a young woman earns 11 cents to sew a pair of Arizona jeans that sell at J. C. Penney for $14.99. Meanwhile, J. C. Penney earned $566 million in profits, almost equal to Nicaragua's annual national budget.' The sweatshop advocacy group explains, 'Sweatshops can be viewed as a product of the global economy. Fuelled by an abundant supply of labour in the global market, capital mobility and free trade, garment industry giants move from country to country, seeking the lowest labour costs and the highest profit, exploiting workers the world over.'

Many different groups are contributing to the anti-sweatshop campaigns at both the national and international level. These groups share a few major goals. Of primary importance among these is a living wage, defined as enough to provide basic living conditions for a family by the standards of the country or area. Another anti-sweatshop campaign goal is better working conditions since many sweatshops pose substantial danger to health and even life, with dangerous equipment, insanitary working conditions and exposure to toxic chemicals. A third important aspect of anti-sweatshop campaigns is the right to organize. Both in America and around the world, garment workers have been denied the right to collective bargaining, often facing sanctions or even being fired if they challenged management. This is a major reason why many unions are joining in the campaigns against sweatshops.

The Jubilee Movement

One of the most exciting campaigns moving across the globe today is called the Jubilee Movement. This call to cancel the unpayable debt that is crushing the world's poorest countries is exciting the imagination of people everywhere. Led by the religious community, Jubilee is drawing very diverse people together to make a moral demand on the leaders of the global economy. Again, religious language and symbols are being employed to attack economic injustice.

Global economic inequality stands today as an increasingly desperate problem for most of the world's people. A major factor in this inequality is poor countries' indebtedness to wealthier countries, which has caused entire nations to declare bankruptcy as the drain on their resources accelerates. A result of this international debt is rapidly degenerating social conditions for the poorest of the poor, as education, health care and the environment continue to deteriorate.

In 1996, the situation's desperateness was finally recognized by donor nations, who responded by creating the Heavily Indebted Poor Countries (HIPC) initiative, which aimed to achieve 'debt sustainability' for the poorest countries. However, religious people worldwide are protesting that debt sustainability is not adequate; they claim that debt cancellation, not management, is the moral imperative. The result is an international campaign known as Jubilee.

This movement draws its inspiration from the book of Leviticus in the Hebrew Scriptures, which calls for a Year of Jubilee every 50 years. In the Jubilee Year, social inequalities are rectified: slaves are freed, land is returned to its original owners, and debts are cancelled. The campaign is now organized in 60 countries, and petitions for debt cancellation are being collected in over 100 nations. Numerous international figures – from Pope John Paul II to U2 lead singer, Bono – support the campaign.

While the international economic crisis has a complex history, it is indisputable that there is a strong correlation between a citizen's poverty and his or her nation's level of indebtedness. Jubilee has marked 52 countries as in desperate need of having their external debt cancelled because of its detrimental effects on their citizens. In 1996, there were 984 million people in these countries; each man, woman and child's average share of the foreign debt was $377 and their annual income was $425! In 31 countries, the per capita share of debt was larger than the per capita annual income.

Using the slogan 'Break the Chains of Debt', organizers around the world have come up with a variety of creative applications of that symbolism. The formation of human chains has become an international symbol. In May 1998, during the annual summit of the G8 heads of state in Birmingham, in the UK, 70,000 people formed a human chain around the city centre meeting location.

Bishop John Davies, one of the participants, reported: 'I got caught up with a group of about sixteen bishops...we walked around about half the chain ending up at St Philip's Cathedral...This procession was an extraordinary experience. As we walked we were greeted all along with deafening cheering, whistles, drums, rattles, as if we were a winning football team...At Birmingham, thousands of people had caught a straight simple enthusiasm for a straight simple idea: whatever the complications and difficulties, it is intolerable to allow the present arrangements of unpayable debt to continue.'

At the height of the event, eight schoolchildren walked around the chain, each carrying a box of petitions and representing a G8 country. They were accompanied by a town crier and a host of bishops, and were greeted with huge cheers from everyone spread out along the chain. They delivered the petitions (a total of 1.5 million signatures) to a summit representative.

Some ask who will pay for the cancelled debt. From a moral point of view, the question is compelling indeed. Consider these facts: The people in the rich countries who made these loans are not poor. The people in the developing countries who received and mostly benefited from those loans are not poor either. But the people who are suffering the most from the burden of the debt are poor. The biblical wisdom, recognizing that such disparities and injustices will occur, calls for periodic debt relief to begin to level the playing field at least a little.

At this stage in the international debt crisis, Jubilee is emerging as a growing moral force in the debate. In the United States, the Jubilee USA campaign was founded in June 1997. While it largely draws from religious organizations, it is not limited to them. Over a hundred major organizations and thousands of individuals have endorsed Jubilee in the United States

The campaign's efforts include education, building consensus, organizing grassroots networks and conducting an advocacy campaign. It held its first national conference in 1998 in Washington, DC, to further develop an education and organizing strategy. People attended the conference from 26 states and several other countries. It concluded with the formation of a human chain around the headquarters of the International Monetary Fund.

During the G8 summit in 1999, over one million people around the world participated in a variety of activities, culminating in human chains in major world capitals. Hundreds of thousands of people circled the meeting place in Cologne, and a petition with over 2 million signatures was handed to the leaders gathered there.

At the Cologne summit, the heads of the creditor nations reached agreement on a plan to triple the debt relief available for the world's poorest nations. The Cologne Debt Initiative provided a significant reduction of debts owed to international creditor agencies by some countries. While Jubilee USA continued to insist on definitive cancellation of crushing debt, without harmful conditions, the campaign strongly believed that full financing of the Cologne Initiative could deliver substantial debt relief for some countries that are desperately in need, as an initial step forward.

Yet financing for full US participation in the Cologne Debt Initiative for fiscal year 2000 faced a major struggle in Congress. The Senate Appropriations Committee initially approved a foreign operations appropriations Bill that included only $75 million for debt relief, although $435 had been requested in order to fulfil the US government's commitment. A grassroots Jubilee campaign swung into action.

Letters and phone calls poured into Congress. On 9 April 2000, a 'Cancel the Debt' rally was held in Washington, DC, culminating with thousands of people forming a human chain around the US Capitol. During the summer, the diversity of the debt relief coalition was on display at a White House meeting as televangelist Pat Robertson and U2 lead singer, Bono, appeared at a press briefing with President Clinton to urge passage of the appropriation. In the autumn, the Congressional leadership finally agreed to fund the full request, and it was signed into law at a White House ceremony attended by many Jubilee representatives.

Sonny Callahan, a ranking member of the House committee that controls the foreign aid budget, was quoted in the *New York Times*: 'The debt relief issue is now a speeding train. We've got the pope and every missionary in the world involved in this thing, and they persuaded just about everyone here that this is the noble thing to do.'

The *Times* reporter noted that the Congressional agreement was 'a sign that street protests and parish activism about the problems of globalization have had an impact on Congress'. And President Clinton proclaimed, 'It's not often we have a chance to do something that economists tell us is a financial imperative and religious leaders say is a moral imperative.'

Following a meeting with Bono, even the arch-conservative Senator Jesse Helms got on board the train. In a *New York Times* interview, Bono said: 'When I met with Senator Jesse Helms, he wept. I talked to him about the biblical origin of the idea of Jubilee Year, the idea that every 49 years, you were supposed to release people from their debt and slaves were supposed to be set free. It's very punk rock for God, but I think it's in Leviticus. He was genuinely moved by the story of the continent of Africa, and he said to me, "America needs to do more." I think he felt it as a burden on a spiritual level.'

It was, as the *Times* story concluded, 'a victory for a coalition of rock stars, religious figures, and charity groups that have made debt forgiveness a moral touchstone for wealthy nations'. And it's yet another example of how a movement of concerned and active people, grounded in moral and religious beliefs, can change the wind to accomplish what only a few short years ago seemed impossible.

The Jubilee movement continues to call for the definitive cancellation of international debt for countries burdened with high levels of human need and environmental distress, in ways that benefit ordinary people and include their participation, and without conditions that perpetuate or deepen poverty. And the growing participation of people around the world is giving a strong momentum to that moral imperative.

Call to Renewal

Call to Renewal seeks to unite churches and faith-based organizations in a biblical commitment to overcome poverty and the problems that fuel it. We want to bring people together for spiritual renewal, social responsibility and moral politics. We help create new networks of cooperation among churches and faith-based organizations at the national and local levels. We build partnerships with other faith traditions, nonprofit organizations, business, labour and government officials. We are forging a unified faith-based and nonpartisan voice on the most critical public issues that affect people who are poor, and, indeed, that might shape a more fair and just society for us all.

As church leaders and organizers have come together, four priorities have emerged:

- Overcoming poverty. We must expand economic opportunity and secure economic justice. Both personal and societal responsibilities are necessary to break the grip of poverty over people's lives.
- Dismantling racism and white privilege in our society. We must commit ourselves to racial justice and reconciliation in our personal lives, our congregations, our neighbourhoods and in the very structures of our society.
- Rebuilding the bonds of healthy families and supportive communities. These hold our society together and, especially, nurture and bring up our children.
- Reasserting the fundamental dignity of each human life. We must commit ourselves to treating every person with the full rights of citizenship and full respect, as being created in the image of God.

The opportunity is real and present. Our nation is experiencing unprecedented economic growth and prosperity, but this economic boom is not being adequately shared – in fact, the income gap between rich and poor continues to grow. The biblical mandate to overcome poverty is clear: the Bible says the ultimate test of a society's integrity in God's eyes is how it treats those who are poor and marginalized. The time has come to answer this moral dilemma with a spiritual charge. Looking both to the biblical imperatives and the societal situation, to avoid danger faith communities must seize the opportunity to step forward and declare, 'If not now, when?'

Call to Renewal is not a new organization; it is a federation with which individuals, local churches, faith-based organizations and national bodies are invited to affiliate. Our intention is not to replace or undermine any existing efforts or institutions but rather to connect and strengthen them, then expand their influence by magnifying their collective voice. Our structure is federated, but our spirituality will be covenantal. We will be bound together in our diversity by a spiritual covenant to act by faith in overcoming poverty. That covenant reads as follows:

The persistence of widespread poverty in our midst is morally unacceptable. Just as some of our religious forebears decided to no longer accept slavery or segregation, we decide to no longer accept poverty. In the biblical tradition, we covenant together in a Call to Renewal. By entering into this Covenant, we commit ourselves to:

1 PRIORITIZE people who are poor – both in our personal, family, and vocational lives and in our congregational and organizational practices – through prayer and dedication of our time and resources.
2 DECIDE our own financial choices in ways that promote economic opportunity and justice for those in poverty.
3 EVALUATE all public policies and political candidates by how they affect people who are poor.
4 CHALLENGE racism, dismantle the structures of racial injustice and white privilege still present, and seek reconciliation among all groups in our society.
5 NURTURE the bonds of family and community and protect the dignity of each person.
6 ORGANIZE across barriers of race, denomination, and social boundaries in common commitment and action to overcome poverty in our own communities, our nation, and our world.

The 'Covenant to Overcome Poverty' was publicly announced on the East steps of the US Capitol on 16 February 2000, by leaders of the nation's churches and church-based organizations, who then committed themselves to a ten-year campaign to implement it. As the *New York Times* wrote, 'Concerned that poverty persists in America despite a prolonged period of national prosperity, a broad group of Christian leaders gathered in Washington yesterday to call for an effort by churches, businesses, labour and government to help poor people.'

The statements from every sector of the church were concise, clear and compelling. John Carr of the US Catholic Conference said, 'Today, the Christian churches come together across denominational and ideological lines to insist we will measure this (election) campaign by how it treats the least of these.' Rich Cizik of the National Association of Evangelicals added: 'There is no way that we can say we are committed to the authoritative Word of God, inspired Scriptures, unless we are committed, I believe, to the cause of the poor.'

The new general secretary of the National Council of Churches, Bob Edgar, concurred by saying, 'It's not too late for people of faith from all traditions – liberal, conservative, and moderate – to covenant together to make sure that within the next few years no child in America has to live in poverty.' And the Revd Wallace Charles Smith spoke for the Progressive National Baptist Convention and testified to the God the black church knows who is 'inside the furnace with the poor, the oppressed, and the afflicted'.

Mark Publow of World Vision, Bread for the World's David Beckmann, and Sharon Daly of Catholic Charities USA added their words of support.

Nearly 70 religious leaders have now signed the Covenant, and are working together on the campaign. The campaign declares that while we do not have a detailed blueprint for overcoming poverty, we can set forth practical goals that a good society should achieve. These goals are:

• a living family income for all who responsibly work
• full participation by people of all races
• affordable, quality health care for all, regardless of income
• schools that work for all our children
• safe, affordable housing

- safe and secure neighbourhoods
- family-friendly policies and programmes in every sector of society

We are committed to each of these goals as a moral priority, and are now working for the concrete policies that can accomplish them.

Already, Call to Renewal has convened the broadest faith-based national roundtables in years around the issue of poverty, and there is Call to Renewal activity in more than 50 cities and local communities, where many are forming local roundtables.

Call to Renewal will stay focused on overcoming poverty and the problems that fuel it, rather than be drawn into debates over theology, doctrine, tradition or other contentious social issues – important issues but not our focus. Our focus and our unity will be on the biblical imperative to overcome poverty. Call to Renewal is a *network* and a *voice* hoping to spark a *movement* – the final subject of this book, to which we will now turn.

Chapter Thirteen

Change the Wind

*Therefore, since we are surrounded by so great a cloud of witnesses,
let us also lay aside every weight and the sin that clings so closely,
and let us run with perseverance the race that is set before us.*
(Hebrews 12.1)

IN WASHINGTON, DC, most of our elected officials suffer a common affliction. I call it the 'wet-finger politician syndrome'. You get it by constantly licking your finger and putting it up in the air to see which way the wind is blowing.

Many people, both inside and outside the capital city, have a similar bad habit when it comes to politics. They have become convinced that you can change things by merely replacing one wet-finger politician with another. Millions of dollars are spent in this pursuit, but nothing much changes.

There is another approach – a better strategy used effectively by the most successful social movements throughout history. It's called *changing the wind*. When you change the wind the politicians will quickly sense it and, remarkably, change their direction too. Moral leaders like Martin Luther King, Jr, and Mahatma Gandhi understood this. To accomplish their bold agendas, they knew their movements would have to change the way people think. The very spiritual climate of the nation would have to be altered. Change the wind, and the necessary political reforms will follow.

For example, the US Congress passed the historic Civil Rights Act in July of 1964. Six months later, after his return from the Nobel Peace Prize ceremonies in Oslo, Dr Martin Luther King, Jr, went to see Lyndon Johnson. The civil rights leader told the president that the country now needed a voting rights Act. He pressed hard for federal action.

But the consummate politician from Texas told the nation's moral leader that a new voting rights law was impossible. Johnson claimed that he had just cashed in all his political chips with the Southern senators to get the Civil Rights Act through Congress and he had no political capital left. But Martin Luther King, Jr, persisted; without the right to vote in the South, blacks could not change their own communities. Lyndon Johnson was the master of political realism. The president said he was sorry, but insisted that it would be five or ten years before it would be possible to achieve voting rights. But King said the nation couldn't wait that long.

Not one to just complain or give up, King began to organize. He chose a sleepy little town of which the world had never heard – Selma, Alabama. A new campaign would be focused there, one that would draw the nation's attention to the moral imperative of gaining the right to vote for America's black citizens. The campaign made Selma internationally famous, and the marches there became a watershed event, just as the Birmingham demonstrations had been before the civil rights law was passed. On 7 March 1965, the 'bloody Sunday' march took civil rights workers across the Edmund Pettus Bridge to confront Sheriff Jim Clark's brutal troopers. On that day, many marchers were badly beaten, including a young man from Atlanta named John Lewis, now a highly respected congressman from Georgia. The very public confrontation galvanized the nation, and on 15 March, President Lyndon Johnson appeared before a joint session of Congress to submit the Voting Rights Act.

On 21 March, the famed Selma-to-Montgomery march took place with the whole nation watching. The nation's religious community mobilized as never before. Hundreds of ministers, white and black, from many denominations across the country, joined civil rights workers and the courageous people of Alabama to make the historic trek. Jewish rabbi Abraham Joshua Heschel marched shoulder to shoulder with Baptist minister Martin Luther King, Jr. The dramatic scene flashed across the nation's consciousness, and the whole world was moved by the moral struggle for political freedom in the American South.

Within five months, Congress passed the historic Voting Rights Act. What was said to be impossible suddenly became possible. On 6 August, President Johnson, with Dr Martin Luther King, Jr, attending the ceremony in the US Capitol Rotunda, signed the Act into law. Selma had altered the calculation of what was politically realistic. King had changed the wind.

The whole history of the civil rights movement demonstrated

the power of the 'outside/inside' strategy that can be most effective in seeking social change. King and others pounded on the doors of power with the persistence of the poor woman in the Gospel story of the widow and the judge. He didn't want to be bothered with her, but she kept knocking on his door until he finally had to open it and pay attention to her honest demands. This time, it was the grassroots movement that attracted the national attention that finally opened the doors of change. Those who want to change the world have to change the way the wind is blowing on the issues they care most about. Don't settle for surface political goals; go for real change, aim at changing the way people think and feel, and the political changes will follow. The stories of successful social movements all prove that.

A New Movement?

I believe we are on the verge of a spiritually based movement for social change. I'm using that word 'movement' deliberately, even daringly. For too long we've been afraid to speak of a movement, ever since the death of Martin Luther King, Jr.

The movement question came up in a conversation I was having with about 50 Denver civic leaders about the relationship between faith and public life. The woman who posed it was a veteran of many social and political campaigns. 'I remember my early days and the feeling of being part of a movement,' she said. 'But we lost that and seem to have got very scattered. I'm wondering if the time has come to refocus our energies, to come together around something. Is that possible?' Her question was deep and heartfelt. The nodding heads from around the room suggested that it was everyone's question, not only people of her generation but young people eager to commit their lives to something that would make a difference.

I answered with my Memphis story. In the autumn of 1996, I was on a whirlwind speaking tour that took me to almost every part of the country. We held 65 town meetings and public events in 34 cities in just seven weeks. It was an organizing tour to unite the churches and local communities around the challenging process of welfare reform and the deeper agenda of overcoming poverty. After our opening conference in Washington, DC, attracted front page coverage in the *New York Times*, the tour moved into high gear.

Near the very end, we arrived in Memphis, tired but buoyed up by the enthusiastic response we had received along the way. Since so much of my personal history is bound up with the civil rights movement, I was especially looking forward to visiting the National Civil Rights Museum, located in what was formerly the Lorraine Motel, the place where Dr King was assassinated. I knew I would be fascinated by the museum, and I was. But it was the very end of the museum tour that I found so startling.

The museum's story of the freedom movement ends in the exact space where Dr King was shot. It's a small glass-enclosed cubicle with two preserved motel rooms on either side: 306 and 307, the rooms where Martin Luther King, Jr, and his colleagues normally stayed. Peering through the glass into Room 306, the last place King would ever sleep, I could see the room just as it had been on that fateful day: the unmade bed, the half-eaten lunch, the open suitcases on the floor. Looking straight ahead, my eyes focused on the balcony, the balcony where Dr King was standing when struck by an assassin's bullet. I slowly approached the edge of the glass, now almost standing on the balcony myself and looking over into the car park where King's young lieutenants – Jesse Jackson, Andrew Young and others – had stood bantering and laughing with their leader. They were all waiting for the Revd Ralph Abernathy, King's longtime friend and co-worker, who was still in the room knotting his tie, so they could all go to dinner at the home of a local clergyman.

All along the inside wall of the glass cubicle is a detailed chronology of the last days and hours of Martin Luther King, Jr. I already knew the story pretty well, but there was much more detail here than I had ever read before. I started at the beginning and carefully read every word, slowly making my way around the little room, pausing every few steps to look again into the two rooms or over the balcony. I remembered how Dr King had called down to Ben Branch, standing in the car park below, 'Ben, would you play "Precious Lord" for me at the meeting tonight?' The piano player responded, 'Dr King, you know I always play "Precious Lord" for you!' King replied, 'I know, Ben, but could you play it especially pretty for me tonight?' Branch responded, 'You know I will, Doctor, you know I will.' Now, in that tiny room at the end of the civil rights museum tour, 'Precious Lord' was playing . . . over and over again.

Precious Lord, take my hand.
Lead me on, let me stand.

The experience was overwhelming. For myself and many others, what happened that day on the balcony became a pivotal moment in our lives. Though I had never been to the Lorraine Motel before, I had visited there many times in my mind and heart. Now I was really there, seeing how it actually was, reading the account of every step and event, listening to the repeated strains of the old gospel hymn.

It was near the end of the inscribed chronicle on the wall that I found something that almost made my heart stand still. In the account of King's last moments, I discovered an exchange of words and emotions I had never read or heard before. After he was shot, the museum's solemn narrative reported, Andrew Young and Ralph Abernathy reached King at about the same time and were both cradling him in their arms as he was dying. Andy Young wailed, 'It's over, it's all over!' But Abernathy rebuked him. 'Don't say that. It's not over; it will never be over.'

I couldn't contain my emotions any longer and felt the tears welling up inside. But a question welled up along with the tears: Who turned out to be right; Young or Abernathy? I sorrowfully concluded that Andrew Young's lament had proven true. As far as the movement was concerned, it was over with the death of Martin Luther King, Jr.

Of course, many powerful things have been done since that sorrowful spring day in 1968. Organizations, projects, campaigns and coalitions have accomplished momentous and truly wonderful deeds. Our own work at Sojourners Community and *Sojourners* magazine was inspired in part by the civil rights movement. But I realized in Memphis that we haven't really dared to speak about movement since then. We've talked more about various rights than about our responsibilities to really change society. Many people have organized around a myriad of individual issues, but we haven't committed ourselves to building a movement for fundamental social change since the day King was killed.

King was in Memphis on behalf of refuse collectors. He was in the midst of constructing a 'poor people's campaign' to address the massive poverty still persistent in the richest nation on earth when he was cut down. Like the prophet he was, King had moved beyond civil rights and was confronting the endemic economic injustice in the land. There was great potential for such a movement, based on the success of the freedom struggle and the new coalitions it had brought into being. But it never happened. The dreamer died, and the poor people's campaign he wanted to begin never got off the ground. When other civil rights leaders tried to bring the campaign to Washington many months later, they were confronted by torrential rains and public indifference. They pitched their tents outside the corridors of power, but the vision of a new poor people's movement just sank in the mud of a Washington monsoon. More than 30 years later, we have never been able to recapture it.

Standing there on the balcony of the Lorraine Motel, I asked myself if the time was right again. After experiencing the public response in 34 very different American cities, I was beginning to feel that it might be. I was feeling the coming together, the new energy, the crossing of boundaries, the feelings of connection between people and places. And after all, the biblical tradition testifies that in the end, the Revd Ralph Abernathy will be proved right: 'It's not over; it will never be over.'

When I finished telling the story, the woman who asked the question nodded her head, and I could see the tears welling up in her eyes too. After the session was over she came up to quietly shake my hand and tell me that the morning was probably going to change her life more than anything in many years.

That's the question. Is there anything worth changing our lives for? That's what a social movement is all about – when enough people decide that there is. As I travel the country today, I hear people asking those questions again. The answers to the questions will have a lot to do with our future.

Perhaps the most powerful thing about a movement is that anybody can be a part of it. It's not just for leaders and certainly not only for politicians, pundits and the politically correct. I put the stress on ordinary people because they are who finally make a difference in real social movements. People come as they are, participate as they can and at any level they are able. Some people in the civil rights movement gave their lives, others risked what they could, many marched, more supported them in other ways, even more spoke out in their own places where they had some voice and more still decided to act and vote in different ways. That's what a movement is, and many people can be part of it, including you.

Think Movement

Thinking movement is the first step: not creating a movement (nobody can really do that) but laying the groundwork for one. Vincent Harding was a leader in the Southern Freedom Movement and a close associate of Martin Luther King, Jr. Now a professor at the Illiff School of Theology in Denver, Colorado, he is an eminent historian of the freedom movement. Harding's book, *There is a River*, on the long history of the black freedom struggle, is a classic. Vincent has also been a wise mentor and elder to me over many years now. When I get impatient with the pace of change, he will say to me, 'You can't start a movement, but you can get ready for one!' My old friend is not hesitant to remind me of the need for such preparation, and that wisdom has often carried me.

On 1 December 1955, Rosa Parks refused to give up her seat on a bus in Montgomery, Alabama, but not just because she was tired. She had been on retreats with other activists, at places like the Highlander Centre in the hills of Tennessee, training and preparing with a network of young African-Americans throughout the South who sensed that history was about to change. They didn't know where, when or how the moment of opportunity would arise, but they wanted to be ready. They felt their times were pregnant with possibilities. Without the preparation from a network of those committed activists and the spiritual base of the black church, there never would have been a civil rights movement. A whole generation of black people in the South were preparing for a movement long before Rosa Parks decided not to give up her seat on the bus. They were motivated by a set of core values – values that would shape a new politics and shake a nation. And the moral appeal of that movement was the ultimate reason why the politics of the civil rights movement succeeded.

I've seen the wind change because of other movements in which I've been involved. In the 1960s, college students changed the way America thought about the war in Vietnam. In the 1970s, determined activists changed the way the whole country thought about the environment and women's rights. In the 1980s, churches made a moral issue of nuclear weapons, US policies in Central America and the nation's abortion rate. And in the 1990s, a handful of organizers led a campaign that caused the United States government to reverse its position and support economic sanctions against South Africa's white regime, an action that became the final straw that broke the back of apartheid. An even smaller group of late-1990s campaigners worked the Internet to turn almost the entire international community against landmines, and won a Nobel Peace Prize for their efforts. In each case, a moral argument changed the wind. Historically, social movements seem to have several characteristics in common.

First, social movements are not just about self-interest, but are about right and wrong. They raise moral issues, not just political ones. Movements involve people by appealing to their best selves, their best visions and their best hopes for their children. They ask what is the right thing to do, the moral thing to do, the Christian thing to do, and so on. For example, the growing social inequality in America and the world doesn't just pose economic challenges but raises fundamental issues of justice, a religious concern. A social movement to address those issues should make the moral questions clear. Recovering the transcendent character of moral values in a rights-based culture is key to the success of any social movement. Don't be afraid to raise the moral issues at the root of the questions you want to address and the things you want to change. It's the best way to mobilize people around a social movement.

Second, minorities, not majorities, always begin movements. Historically, it has usually been committed minorities, acting on moral concerns, that bring issues to public consciousness. Minorities catalyse the situation, establish new agendas and succeed, finally, when majorities choose not to oppose them. If they win the majority's agreement, it's usually owing to the moral force as well as the political logic of their argument. Majorities seldom become involved, but they eventually agree to the proposed changes, or at least decide not to resist them. It is minorities that change the terms of public debate; majorities just watch the discussion. The late anthropologist Margaret Mead said it well: 'Don't think that small groups of people can't change the world; they're the only ones who ever have.' That means you don't have to convince the majority in your church, neighbourhood or nation before you begin to act. All you need is a committed and motivated minority in order to begin.

Third, action changes the terms of the public debate. Discussion is usually not enough. It takes action to get people's attention. From the biblical prophets to the great social movements we've discussed to the many examples I've cited of what people are doing today in their local communities, it's taking action that *creates* a new dialogue. After a public action has been taken and people have seen it, the discussion about the issues at stake becomes a public one. Until that point, there might have been many private conversations, but nothing had brought the issue out into the open. Action has the power to do that. It often takes action on the part of some individual or group (much better if it's a group) to make a community or a society deal with something they haven't dealt with before. So don't just sit around talking for ever about your concerns. Find a way to take action, the more creative and courageous the better.

Fourth, movements make the connection between the personal and the social. In building social movements, it's not that self-interest is unimportant but rather that it gets redefined. Perhaps the most important question a movement can ask is who the 'we' is. I give a sermon along these lines. I ask the audience to consider how wide their circle is, who's part of the family, who's in and who's out, and who is it that we're fighting for? It's a critical question. The best movements are those that enable people to connect their own self-interest to the interests of others. We are most satisfied when we feel part of something larger than ourselves. In a movement, self-interest becomes engaged in a larger common interest, and personal agendas become shaped by the common good. In your own situation, ask how you can connect people's personal interests to the problems at stake in the community. Find ways for the interests of the community to intersect with the personal and family concerns in people's hearts. You'll give people a larger purpose and find it creates both satisfaction and fulfilment.

Fifth, movements develop inclusive agendas. For example, social inequality and the pressures of a global economy don't impact poor people only. There is enormous pain in our middle-class neighbourhoods and churches, where people are trying to hold their jobs and their families together, not to mention find time for significant involvement in wider community activities. We know that many single parents are not making it, but many two-parent families are also struggling just to keep up. Economics, family and community are not coming together for millions of people today. A good society would want to support all three and keep them in balance. But we've lost our balance. Many people are hurting, and they're not all poor, and taking seriously the depth of that social and economic pain is crucial to building a movement for economic justice. Calls to help the poor may sound like just another demand for time and money from people who feel they have less and less of both. People who feel squeezed normally don't feel generous. But if the call can be framed in the context of the common good, asking what we all need and putting forward a vision of economics, family and community that might work better for *everyone*, including the poor, it will come across much more effectively. Ask yourself what some of the issues are that will bring in many people. How can we connect the needs of the poor with the needs and well-being of the wider community?

Sixth, movements are visionary. The role of a movement, especially one that is spiritually or religiously based, should be to offer a vision for what society should be or do. What kind of country do we want to be, and what should our nation mean to the rest of the world? Those are the kinds of questions a movement asks. Such questions also help people understand themselves as a democratic people, not just as cogs in a world of economic determinism. We are asked to set aside the relentless demands of technology and the global economy for a moment, and to consider the larger questions of what we want as a nation and what quality and style of life we are trying to achieve. Those seeking a new vision talk about covenants, they make compacts, they pledge commitments. Movements speak a moral language that calls us back to the things we value most, which helps us remember that there are things we regard as more important than the pressures of our daily lives. Social change movements don't seek volunteers just to make the present more tolerable; they recruit members who together take a stance for a better future. Movements talk past the present and imagine a new future. The only way you can do that is to assert moral agency and responsibility in the midst of assumptions and structures that militate against both. Moral claims are made on social conditions, and that becomes a matter of faith. While both secular therapists and religious pietists encourage their clients and converts to seek private solutions to social problems, movements invite people to find public solutions as well. So don't just spend your time volunteering and filling up your life with social service; instead join with others around a real vision for changing something important.

Seventh, movements are prophetic. Religious communities and people of faith have played a key role in starting and sustaining social movements, as we have noted throughout this book. Abolition of slavery, civil rights, women's suffrage, child protection, labour laws, peace and human rights were all movements that relied heavily on the participation of communities motivated by spiritual values. There are good reasons for that. Religious communities have the capacity to create movements precisely because of their belief systems. None of the above causes were ready to become part of the governing politics of their times when they first became social movements. In other words, movement politics never start with electoral politics. Rather, they begin to raise a public voice that, over time, politicians will be unable to ignore. Many social movements begin by asserting a moral claim or vision as an article of faith. Economic justice, for example, is a tenet of biblical faith just as are many other religious doctrines. It remains a tenet of faith whether or not the economic boom pays any attention to it, or whether or not it is possible today to immediately create an economy that is more just and fair. If the Bible says that economic injustice should be corrected and massive inequalities require periodic redistribution of wealth, that's enough to undergird and motivate a spiritual movement.

The civil rights movement didn't begin in Selma. Black churches were protesting lynchings at the turn of the century, developing leadership, protecting the community in numerous ways, supporting the legal battles of the National Association for the Advancement of Colored People (NAACP), and much more. It wasn't a surprise when many black churches became the institutional support bases for the civil rights movement. It is the job of faith communities to put issues on the public agenda long before they can be achieved. But putting them on the agenda is the beginning of the long process that leads to eventual victory. So don't be intimidated by somebody else's political realism. Be willing to make a bold faith statement and put something on the agenda as the first step toward making it happen.

Ask yourself how the attributes of the social movements described above apply to your own personal involvements or the organizations you work with. Are you just thinking about volunteering or are you thinking movement? Are they just thinking about service, or are they thinking about a movement for social change?

What If?

Today, the moral case is growing for dealing with the unfinished agenda of overcoming poverty in the wealthiest country in the world and addressing the tremendous gulf between the so-called developed and developing worlds. In particular, the fate of millions of children, whom we have talked about throughout this book, is becoming a common focus.

As we have seen, a new unity in the religious community concerning poverty promises to provide the leadership that we have lacked. In many quarters, the commitment to connect economics to moral concerns is growing. But this would probably not become a movement if it were focused only on the poor. Because the issues of economic fairness touch the lives of so many people today, and because the moral questions at stake have to do with the well-being of our very souls, many different kinds of people are becoming involved.

Many Americans are feeling the need for a spiritual renewal of democracy itself, whose soul is also in crisis, as evidenced by the dramatic decline of voter participation in US elections. If democracy is to be renewed in our time, if the poor are to be included in the mainstream of our society and treated more fairly around the world, and if the middle class is to find a purpose deeper than shopping, we will need to change the wind and alter our moral framework. Only a more spiritual language can renew our society and accomplish these things. We need to make the spiritual connections between the great issues of our time, while linking real solutions to the best moral values of both our religious and our political traditions. Only then will the wind begin to change.

In the 1960s, the country finally agreed that black people in America should be equal citizens under the law. When Dr Martin Luther King, Jr, was assassinated in 1968, the agenda of establishing basic civil rights for all Americans, regardless of race, had been substantially accomplished. But the new mission to which he had turned his attention – to confront the massive poverty of American society – had hardly begun. That agenda remains unfinished.

For too long, efforts to relieve poverty in America have often been halfhearted and ill conceived. The great ideological debate between liberals and conservatives over social entitlement versus personal responsibility has left us incapable of acting. The practical result of that tired debate has produced a societal schizophrenia gravitating between substandard maintenance or neglectful abandonment of the lives of America's most vulnerable families, predominantly women and children.

Now the nation must decide whether its poorest, youngest and most vulnerable citizens are part of the nation and the economy. That will require a change in the wind, but it's something we can do. And it's something you can help to accomplish. Don't be daunted by the task; it's only by joining together that we will change the wind. In the words of the biblical writer of the Book of Hebrews, we are invited to 'lay aside every weight...and run the race that is set before us'.

The task of overcoming poverty is a spiritual one. The call is to renewal – in our personal and family lives, in our congregations, in our neighbourhoods and cities, and in our nation. For all of us, it is a matter of civic responsibility to make sure our poorest citizens are not left behind. For biblical people it is a matter of obedience to the admonition of the prophet Micah to 'do justice, love kindness, and walk humbly with your God'. For Christians, it is a matter of discipleship to Jesus Christ, who reminds us 'as you have done it to the least of these, you have done it to me'.

What if poor people finally got our attention? What if we started also paying attention to what the Bible says about wealth and poverty? What if we decided to include the bottom 25 per cent of Americans and their 15 million children in our society? What if we stopped arguing about the many reasons why people are poor and instead began focusing our collective energies on really overcoming poverty? What if we called off the old debates about welfare (since the government is all but ending it anyway) and instead pulled together to assist poor families in making the difficult passage from welfare and poverty to work, dignity and community? What if we started moving beyond just providing services for poor people to actually helping them move out of poverty? What if we stopped talking about 'the poor' and instead started including everybody in 'the community'?

What if we stopped making the false choices that have impoverished our political debate and failed to resolve the vexing issues of poverty? And what if we replaced false choices with critical connections between good values and good jobs, between personal responsibility and social justice, between rebuilding families and rebuilding neighbourhoods, between good parenting and liveable family wages, between individual moral choices and governmental responsibility?

What if poor people brought the churches back together again? What if that new unity in the religious community could lead the way for the rest of the society by making an irresistible moral argument for including those at the bottom in the mainstream? What if we stopped arguing about government solutions and private charity and instead formed new partnerships between government, business, labour, churches and other nonprofit organizations in each of our local communities, based on the principle of all people doing their fair share and doing what they do best?

What if we accepted the reality that both conservatives and liberals have useful insights about the complex causes of poverty, but that real solutions will challenge them both? What if people across the political spectrum could jointly get on with the task of improving the quality of life for our poorest, youngest and most vulnerable citizens? What if we replaced the dysfunctional categories of Left and Right, liberal and conservative, with two new questions: What's right and what works? What if we declared that the cold war over poverty is finished?

A Statement of Faith

I've said that movements are built on statements of faith. So I'm going to end this book by making one. *I believe we are on the verge of a new movement for economic justice, led in large part by communities of faith.* To make such a prediction today is certainly a faith statement. But remember, that's how movements begin. And your involvement just might make the critical difference.

Allow me to conclude with a new-father story. When Joy was pregnant, she told me one night in bed that according to all the books, the child in her womb could hear us talking right then. I instinctively leaned down to her pregnant belly and said, 'Luke, hope is believing in spite of the evidence, then watching the evidence change. That's my best line, Luke, and one day you'll discover that it's true.' It is my best line and, in the days ahead, I hope we all discover how true it is.

Notes

INTRODUCTION The Difference That Faith Makes

page

xxi   Biblical definition of 'faith' from Hebrews 11.1.

xxiv   For the history of the US civil rights movement, see Taylor Branch, *Parting the Waters* (New York: Simon and Schuster, 1988) and *Pillar of Fire* (New York: Simon and Schuster, 1998); and David Garrow, *Bearing the Cross* (New York: William Morrow, 1986).

xxiv–xxv For the story of the South African struggle against apartheid, see Nelson Mandela, *Long Walk to Freedom* (London; Little, Brown, 1994) and Desmond Tutu, *The Rainbow People of God* (New York: Doubleday, 1994).

CHAPTER ONE Trust Your Questions

4   William E. Pannell, *My Friend, the Enemy* (Waco: Word Books, 1968).

6   *Report of the National Advisory Commission on Civil Disorders* (Kerner Report) (New York: Bantam Books, 1968).

6   Malcolm X, with Alex Haley, *The Autobiography of Malcolm X* (New York: Grove Press, 1965).

8   Martin Luther King quote from a speech titled 'Why I Oppose the War', 16 April 1967.

15   Quote from Rich Cizik of the National Association of

Evangelicals, in 'Christian Groups Seek Unity in Fight Against Poverty' by Carlye Murphy, *Washington Post*, 18 October 1997.

CHAPTER TWO Get Out of the House More Often

19   Estimates that 5 million people, including 2.5 million children, die from unsafe drinking water and sanitation, from World Health Organization, www.who.org.

20   Story of Olga from Joe Nangle, 'The Nature of God', *Sojourners*, July/August 1998.

20–21   Dale S. Recinella, 'What's in a Name?'

CHAPTER THREE Use Your Gift

33   Cost figures for Christ House and DC hospital system from Christ House, 1717 Columbia Rd, NW, Washington, DC, 20009.

36–37   Sojourners Neighborhood Center mural, in *Washington Post*, 2 August 1990.

38   Hillel quote from *Pirke Aboth* (Sayings of the Fathers), I. 14.

38–40   Marshall Ganz story on David and Goliath from a talk given at a labour retreat, 24 May 1999.

40–41   For the Sing Sing story, see Hans Hallundbaek, 'Stone Upon Stone', *Sojourners*, March/April 1999.

CHAPTER FOUR Do the Work and You'll Find the Spirit

44   Robert Putnam, 'Bowling Alone', *Journal of Democracy* 6:1, January 1995.

CHAPTER FIVE Recognize the Three Faces of Poverty

52   Michael Harrington, *The Other America* (New York: Macmillan, 1962).

54   Peter Wehner, 'Woe to You Who Are Rich', *The Washington Post*, 12 January 1997.

55   Rep. Tony Hall from Call to Renewal videotape of Capitol Preach-in, 1 June 1998.

58   On distribution of wealth, see *Shifting Fortunes*, p. 6 (from Edward Wolff, 'Recent Trends in Wealth Ownership,' December 1998.

58   United Nations Human Development Report, 'Human Development Report 1998', www.undp.org/hdro/98.htm.

59   United Nations Development Programme, 'Human Development Report 1997'. Press release 'Extreme Poverty Could Be Banished from Globe by Early Next Century, According to Latest Human Development Report', UNDP, 12 June 1997, www.undp.org/news/HDR97/prl-eng.htm.

59   Michael Eisner ($97,000 per hour) and Disney worker in Haiti (28 cents per hour) from National Labor Committee/People of Faith Network Disney Campaign, 1997.

      Michael Jordan making more from Nike than all Asian workers combined, from Richard Barnet, *The Global War Against the Poor* (Washington, DC: Servant Leadership Press).

62   Gandhi's Seven Deadly Sins from Arun Gandhi of the M. K. Gandhi Institute for the Study of Nonviolence: 'The seven deadly sins...were part of my lessons when I lived with Grandfather in 1945–46 as a boy of 12. He made me, and other children in the ashram, memorize them...I don't know if there is any source you can attribute this list to.'

64–65 John DiIulio manuscript, 'Moral Poverty, Churches, and the Inner City'.

CHAPTER SIX Listen to Those Closest to the Problem

72   The Revd Eugene Rivers and Ten Point Coalition, Anthony A. Parker, 'Salvation in the Streets', *Sojourners*, May 1993. See also Eugene F. Rivers, 'Take Your Inheritance: The Challenge Before the Churches', *Sojourners*, February–March, 1994.

74   The Revd Jeff Brown quote from personal conversation with the author.

74   The Revd Ray Hammond quote from personal conversation with the author.

      The Revd Jeff Brown quote from statement at Call to Renewal press conference, National Press Club, Washington, DC, 16 December 1997.

77–81 On Bethel New Life and Mary Nelson, see Kevin Clarke, 'Leaven in the Loaf', *Sojourners*, November–December 1998. Additional information from Mary Nelson.

81   Isaiah 65.21–23 and Micah 4.4.

83–84 Tom Jones quote from personal letter, 4 January 1999.

CHAPTER SEVEN Get to the Heart of the Matter

88   *Entertaining Angels: The Dorothy Day Story*, directed by
           Michael Ray Rhodes, produced by Ellwood E. Kieser, OSP;
           Paulist Pictures, 1996.
89–90   'The Market and the Common Good': Portions of this
           section appeared on MSNBC Online, 'Happy Holidays –
           You're Fired', by Jim Wallis, 16 December 1998.

CHAPTER EIGHT Keep Your Eyes on the Prize

99   Luis E. Lugo, 'Equal Partners: The Welfare Responsibility
           of Governments and Churches', (Washington, DC: Center
           for Public Justice, 1998).
99   The Catechism of the Catholic Church (Washington, DC:
           United States Catholic Conference, 1994).
102   Prime Minister Tony Blair speech, 29 March 2001,
           www.christiansocialist.org.uk/csmnet/blair29_3.doc.
105   Martin Luther King, 'conscience of the state', *The Strength
           to Love* (1963), in *A Testament of Hope*, ed. James M.
           Washington (New York: Harper & Row, 1986), p. 501.

CHAPTER NINE Tap the Power of Faith Communities

107   Garry Wills quotes from *Under God: Religion and
           American Politics* (New York: Simon and Schuster/
           Touchstone, 1990), pp. 16 and 25.
108   David Schribman, 'One Nation Under God: How the
           Religious Right Changed the American Conversation', the
           Boston Globe magazine, 10 January 1999.
111   ˉ   View that churches should spend more time helping the
           poor, 'God and Society in North America: A Survey of
           Religion, Politics, and Social Involvement in Canada and
           the United States', The Angus Reid Group.
112   Joe Klein, 'In God They Trust', *New Yorker*, 16 June 1997.
              Naomi Wolf, 'Onward Christian Hippies', *George*,
           December 1997.
113   Number of Muslims, Buddhists, Hindus from David
           Barrett, *World Christian Encyclopedia* (Oxford University
           Press, 2001).
113–14   Ron Thiemann on 'pilgrim discipleship' from a discussion
           at Harvard Divinity School.
114   For the William Wilberforce story, see Christopher D.
           Hancock, 'The "Shrimp" Who Stopped Slavery', *Christian
           History* 16, no. 1, 1997.

Notes

189

| 128 | Eugene Rivers quote from Call to Renewal National Summit, February 1999. |
| 130 | Marshall Ganz quote from personal correspondence with the author. |

CHAPTER TEN Be a Contemplative

133–34	Nelson Mandela quote from speech at Harvard University.
134	Richard Rohr 'lessons of life' from 'Boys to Men: Rediscovering Rites of Passage for Our Time', *Sojourners*, May/June 1998.
137–38	On Nelson Mandela being awarded the Congressional Gold Medal, see Francis X. Clines, 'The Great Conciliator at the Capital', *The New York Times*, 24 September 1998. Mandela quote from speech to UN General Assembly, 21 September 1998.
139	For editorial comment, see Jim Wallis and Wes Granberg-Michaelson, 'The Nature of Leadership and Personal Vulnerabilities', *Chicago Tribune*, 25 February 1998.
142–43	Henri Nouwen quotes are from *The Road to Peace*, ed. John Dear (Maryknoll, NY: Orbis Books, 1998). The 'three disciplines', from an interview first published in *Alive* magazine, November/December 1994. Central America from 'Christ of the Americas'.
145–46	'A Letter to a Young Activist', Thomas Merton, in *The Hidden Ground of Love* (New York: Farrar, Straus and Giroux, 1985).

CHAPTER ELEVEN Keep it Human

| 151 | Wedding story from *Daily Mail*, 27 October 1997. |
| 153 | Capitol Rotunda story from Francis X. Clines, 'Christians Against Welfare Cuts Are Arrested in Capitol', *New York Times*, 8 December 1995; and Lynn Neary, 'All Things Considered', National Public Radio, 7 December 1995. |

CHAPTER TWELVE Have a Dream

158	US children in poverty figures from 'Poverty in the United States 1999', US Census Bureau, September 2000.
158	Child poverty statistics from Cornel West at 'The Future of American Progressivism', a forum at Harvard, autumn 1998.
160	People of Faith Network information from People of Faith Network, 85 South Oxford Street, Brooklyn, NY 11217.

161 GAO definition from www.sweatshopwatch.org/swatch/industry.

161 Department of Labor quote/estimate from *Los Angeles Times*, 1996, and article in *San Jose Mercury News*, 1 June 1999.

161 Samuel Guerra quote from www.sweatshopwatch.org/swatch/industry/cal/assembly.html.

161 Sweatshop Watch information from 'What is a Sweatshop?', www.sweatshopwatch.org.

161 Co-op America quote from www.sweatshops.org.

163 52 countries and debt statistics from www.oneworld.org/jubilee/jubilee2000/main.html.

163 Birmingham anecdote and Bishop John Davies quote from Jubilee 2000.

165 'Speeding train' from Joseph Kahn, 'Congressional Leadership Agrees to Debt Relief for Poor Nations', *New York Times*, 18 October 2000.

165 Interview with Bono from Susan Dominus, 'The Way We Live Now: Questions for Bono', *New York Times* magazine, 8 October 2000.

166 Call to Renewal mission and four priorities from Call to Renewal Mission Statement.

167 Call to Renewal Covenant from Call to Renewal, 2401 15th St, NW, Washington, DC 2000.

168 Covenant signing see Gustav Niebuhr, 'Christians Ask Renewed Attack on Poverty', *New York Times*, 17 February 2000.

CHAPTER THIRTEEN Change the Wind

171–72 For the story of Martin Luther King, Lyndon Johnson, Selma and the Voting Rights Act see Stephen Oates, *Let the Trumpet Sound* (New York: Harper and Row, 1982), pp. 322–64, 370; and Garrow, *Bearing the Cross*, pp. 368–412.

173 'Colorado Conversations on Renewal', sponsored by the Colorado Civic League, 31 July–1 August 1998. See *Denver Post*, 1 August 1998.

173 The *New York Times* front-page story on the Call to Renewal conference was 'A Religious Tilt Toward the Left', by Francis X. Clines, 16 September 1996.

175 For the Young/Abernathy story, see also Oates, *Let the Trumpet Sound*, pp. 488–90.

175   'Precious Lord' was written by the famed gospel singer/composer Thomas A. Dorsey in 1932 following the death of his wife and baby. It was a favourite song of Dr Martin Luther King, Jr, and gained even greater recognition after Mahalia Jackson sang it at Dr King's funeral. See 'The Precious Legacy of Thomas Dorsey', by Bernice Johnson Reagon, *Washington Post*, 31 January 1993.

177   Vincent Harding, *There is a River* (New York: Harcourt Brace Jovanovich, 1981).

183   Quotes from Scripture:
'lay aside every weight...', Hebrews 12.1.
'do justice...', Micah 6.8.
'...you have done it to me', Matthew 25.40.

Index